Directing

Christopher Bessette

PEDRO ALMODÓVAR

OLIVIER ASSAYAS

SUSANNE BIER

INGMAR BERGMAN

NURI BILGE CEYLAN

JEAN-PIERRE DARDENNE

LUC DARDENNE

GUILLERMO DEL TORO

JOHN FORD

CLINT EASTWOOD

STEPHEN FREARS

TERRY GILLIAM

JEAN-LUC GODARD

AMOS GITAI

PAUL GREENGRASS

MICHAEL HANEKE

ALFRED HITCHCOCK

PARK CHAN-WOOK

ISTVÁN SZABÓ

PETER WEIR

ZHANG YIMOU

AKIRA KUROSAWA

FilmCraft

Directing

Mike Goodridge

AMSTERDAM • BOSTON • HEIDELBERG • LONDON
NEW YORK • OXFORD • PARIS • SAN DIEGO
SAN FRANCISCO • SINGAPORE • SYDNEY • TOKYO
Focal Press is an imprint of Elsevier

Focal Press is an imprint of Elsevier Inc.
225 Wyman Street, Waltham
MA 02451, USA
Copyright © 2012 The Ilex Press Ltd.
All rights reserved

This book was conceived, designed, and produced by
Ilex Press Limited, 210 High Street, Lewes, BN7 2NS, UK

Publisher: Alastair Campbell
Associate Publisher: Adam Juniper
Managing Editors: Natalia Price-Cabrera and Zara Larcombe
Editor: Tara Gallagher
Specialist Editor: Frank Gallaugher
Creative Director: James Hollywell
Senior Designer: Kate Haynes
Design: Grade Design
Picture Manager: Katie Greenwood
Color Origination: Ivy Press Reprographics

Library of Congress Control Number:
A catalog record for this book is available from the
Library of Congress.

ISBN: 978-0-240-81858-0
For information on all Focal Press publications visit our website at:
www.focalpress.com
Printed and bound in China
10 9 8 7 6 5 4 3 2 1

Table of Contents

Introduction

The *FilmCraft* series is designed to explore each of the film crafts through interviews with some of their greatest practitioners, and the first books in the collection, *Cinematography*, *Editing*, and *Costume Design*, have done just that. The directing book, however, presented a variety of additional challenges because directing, perhaps the greatest of the crafts in this collaborative art form, encompasses direction of all the crafts as they relate to the thematic and stylistic essence of the entire enterprise. To encapsulate the craft of sixteen directors in this book is to illustrate the complete process of filmmaking.

The buck stops with the director, of course. If the film works, he or she will be the first to receive acclaim; if it fails, he or she will be blamed for that failure. The pressure on a director throughout the process is enormous. On set the director has not only to realize his or her vision as it was conceived, but to answer every question, put out every fire, respond to the performance as it happens, ensure that the dialogue rings true, and guarantee that there is enough coverage for the edit. In post-production, the director works with the editor to put it all together with the myriad possibilities the digital editing process allows, overseeing sound, music and dubbing, and appeasing financiers anxious that the finished product will please audiences. Filmmaking is as grueling and intensive as it is exhilarating. While actors and crew move on to their next projects, sometimes making two or three films a year, most directors take two years or more to finish one film, unless you are Woody Allen or Michael Winterbottom, whose prodigious outputs are anomalous.

Is it any wonder that the director has to have an ego? For at least a year or two, and sometimes a lot longer, a director has to believe his or her vision in a project and keep it alive and intact while the process itself and the hundreds of people involved often attempt to chip away at its integrity. Filmmaking therefore requires the stubbornness of a mule, but it also demands that the director listen to those around who can make valuable contributions or positive changes. And during production at least, the filmmaker dictates the mood of the set, has the final word on a multitude of day-to-day decisions, and is required to manage a company of people usually larger than most businesses.

Choosing sixteen filmmakers for this book was no easy feat. I wanted a range of styles and nationalities; I wanted some writer/directors—or classic "auteurs," if you like—and some directors who take on existing screenplays and make the projects their own. I wanted some filmmakers who had been working for many decades and some with just a few outstanding films under their belt. I wanted some who are the darlings of the arthouse circuit and some whose films would happily sit on three screens of a multiplex.

The pleasure in the experience of talking with such a variety of filmmakers is that they are all vastly different personalities with different ways of making movies, while their goals remain pretty much the same. Authenticity, whether contextual or emotional, is clearly the ideal—and that is all within the construct of each film, so Guillermo del Toro is as determined that his monsters appear authentic in the troll market in **Hellboy II: The Golden Army** as much as Paul Greengrass wants to recreate the hijacking of Flight United 93 with as much literal detail as he can muster. Susanne Bier talks of her "bullshit detector," which ensures that every nuance of the performance and dialogue in her intense dramas ring true, and Peter Weir describes the reduction of the crucial farewell scene in **Witness** from over-written Hollywood gushing to a simple, unspoken goodbye. Of course, a kind of authenticity is just one element in the patchwork of intent.

Every director has his or her own distinct approach. When you're watching a clip from a Pedro Almodóvar film, you know within seconds that you are watching his work because of the characteristic mise-en-scène, design and colors, the familiar actors, delicious dialogue and score. On the other hand, France's Olivier Assayas is no less an auteur than Almodóvar, but it is not easy to call an Assayas film: this, after all, is the man who made the visceral action epic **Carlos**, the meticulous costume drama **Les destinées sentimentales**, the cyber-sex thriller **Demonlover**, and the languorous French chamber piece **Summer Hours**. His personality is less an obvious factor in his work.

Some of the filmmakers like Peter Weir, Guillermo del Toro, Terry Gilliam and Paul Greengrass have flipped in and out of the Hollywood studio system, making films as broad as **Dead Poets Society** or the Bourne and Hellboy films. But they are all practiced at maintaining their visions while working within the mainstream studio system. Others in the book probably couldn't survive within those parameters. When I spoke to him, Del Toro was in Canada in pre-production on his latest megapicture, an aliens-versus-robots movie called **Pacific Rim**, which has already been set for release as a tent-pole picture in summer 2013. You can hardly imagine the Dardennes or Nuri Bilge Ceylan even knowing what to do on a film of that type or scale. Does that make Del Toro less of an auteur? On the contrary. He is a different breed of director, who can move between smaller, more intimate films like **The Devil's Backbone** and **Pan's Labyrinth**, and large-scale epics for which he has the ambition and aptitude. Zhang Yimou is similar: the same voice behind the glorious simplicity of **The Story Of Qiu Ju** or **Not One Less** can also command a cast of thousands for Chinese blockbusters like **Hero** or his latest film **The Flowers of War**, which cost $90m to produce.

Many of the directors explained that their work is explicitly informed by their upbringing and nationality. István Szabó finds himself repeatedly returning to the turmoil in central Europe in the 20th century; Almodóvar found his voice as the pioneer of a new kind of bold cinema in the years after Franco's death in Spain; Peter Weir describes himself influenced by a trip he took by sea from his native Australia to the UK in his twenties and how it informed his view of the world; the Dardenne brothers continue to make their unique brand of cinema in the familiar surroundings of their home town of Seraing in the region of Liege in Belgium and have no desire to leave; Amos Gitai continues to base his prolific output of work around themes and settings pertaining to Israel and the journey of the Jewish people; Zhang Yimou has spent his entire career in the often restrictive Chinese state film system, sometimes in favor, sometimes out of it.

Even in the process of putting this book together, I have been repeatedly asked how

I chose who I chose. Ultimately, I went after filmmakers behind some of the most extraordinary, or at least my favorite, films in the recent past—**Oldboy**, **Carlos** and **Summer Hours**, **Distant** and **Climates**, **L'enfant** and **The Kid with a Bike**, **Kippur** and **Kadosh**, **Open Hearts** and **After the Wedding**. For others with longer careers, it is their entire oeuvres and the consistency of their output that attracted me: Clint Eastwood, Pedro Almodóvar, Michael Haneke, Zhang Yimou, Stephen Frears. Still others—Del Toro and Gilliam—are just visionaries, whose imaginations are inspiring.

Of course, the selection of the subjects of this book is not an attempt to name the greatest filmmakers at work today. The idea is not that the reader questions the selection and asks why Martin Scorsese isn't included, or Steven Spielberg or David Cronenberg. To some extent, my choices were governed by my desire for diversity, and some of my targeted choices were unavailable in the time frame I had available. Wong Kar-wai, a personal favorite of mine, for example, was involved in another of his laborious post-production periods on **The Grandmasters**—and when Wong is working, there is no disturbing him.

Having said that, I do believe I captured some of the living greats like Eastwood, Almodóvar, Haneke and Zhang Yimou, while giving voice to masters who may not have as large a body of work as those names, but whose genius is apparent—Ceylan from Turkey and the Dardenne brothers from Belgium, for example.

In asking the directors to discuss their craft, it became clear to me early on in the process that their craft only evolved over some years from their first experiences with film. Their personal stories of starting out could perhaps be the most illuminating aspect in the development of their unique talents. Guillermo del Toro talks about how he worked for twelve years on film and TV sets as everything from camera grip to stunt driver before directing **Cronos**. Paul Greengrass talks with passion about the decade he spent making television documentaries for iconic UK series **World In Action**, which acted as the launch pad for his style of making narrative films; the Dardennes also come from a documentary →

background, which goes some way to inform their style of extreme naturalism. Susanne Bier remembers how she made five popular commercial films in Denmark before finding her filmmaking style in **Open Hearts** many years later.

It's perhaps telling that all the subjects required practice making films before they found their groove, a fact that many young filmmakers in today's tough marketplace might envy. They were all allowed to make mistakes, they did make mistakes and they learned from them. It's refreshing to hear the Dardennes, Park Chan-wook and Susanne Bier talking about what went wrong with some of their earliest films, or Stephen Frears discussing why **Mary Reilly** didn't work.

And this being a series looking at all the film crafts, I found it reassuring that the directors interviewed spoke at length and with great sincerity about their closest collaborators, be they actors, writers, cinematographers, or producers. Frears, for example, can't understand why other directors wouldn't have the film's writer on set, as he insists. Szabó's admiration and respect for his actors is palpable, and he enthusiastically welcomes their contributions. Assayas talks at length about the cinematographers with whom he works repeatedly and how each brings different input to the films. Bier discusses the nuts and bolts of her collaboration with writer Anders Thomas Jensen, and how their complicated webs of emotional turmoil are spun together. And Clint Eastwood relies on a team of department heads with whom he has worked for many films, bringing a fluency and ease to his filmmaking that he relishes.

Nobody I interviewed displayed the hubris or arrogance that is often associated with a stereotype of a director. These expert filmmakers most of all exercise a determined passion to tell intriguing stories as well as they can. Compromise, caused by shortage of money, time or light, is inevitable, but as they regularly describe, can usually make for a far more interesting solution.

I asked all the directors to offer their advice to aspiring young filmmakers today and they each came up with different advice to follow. There are

no blueprints. Most of the chapters explore how the directors themselves made their first strides into filmmaking and they all followed individual paths to become the artists they are today. This cannot be replicated. There is no manual that can tell you how to be Almodóvar or Haneke.

But by reading the words of the sixteen filmmakers, readers can glean some insight into what informs their creative choices and how these great storytellers have been formed and continue to evolve. Talking to them and listening to stories and illustrations of how they make films enthralled me, and they have graciously provided us with visual materials here to illustrate some of the processes behind the craft.

Some plan their films with calculated precision, like Michael Haneke, who goes so far as to plot his shot plans at screenplay stage or Park Chan-wook, who storyboards his movies in detail and rarely breaks from the original plan. But even those directors are happy to respond to the surprises of performance or location and Park's most celebrated fight sequence—the corridor combat in **Oldboy**—was thought up on the fly when he abandoned the original elaborate sequence.

Other filmmakers wait until being on set to determine what to shoot. Not that they are any less prepared than Haneke or Park, but they want to respond more readily to the dynamics of the set without exact ideas. Assayas, for example, shot the five-and-a-half-hour **Carlos** in just 92 days, and prides himself on the speed and volume of footage that was shot every day, as well as the improvisation employed by both filmmaker and actors on set. "Chaos is the filmmaker's best ally," he told me.

If you think it was difficult to settle on sixteen of today's most intriguing filmmakers, you can imagine how hard it was to determine the five filmmakers to be represented in our Legacy chapters, which profile innovators and pioneers in the filmmaking field. It's an almost impossible task to single out five directors who have had more influence or broken more ground than others, but the exercise had to be done, and I chose Kurosawa, Bergman, Ford, Hitchcock, and Godard to represent the first 115 years of cinema. I appreciate how many geniuses didn't make this arbitrary and personal shortlist, but among those I also wanted to include were Yasujirô Ozu, Carl Theodor Dreyer, Sergei Eisenstein, Michael Powell, Federico Fellini, Stanley Kubrick, Pier Paolo Pasolini, Luis Buñuel, Michelangelo Antonioni, Charlie Chaplin, Billy Wilder, Jean Renoir, François Truffaut, Douglas Sirk, Satyajit Ray, to name but a few… The list is a long one.

In addition I wanted to mention that, although Susanne Bier is the only woman in the sixteen filmmakers here, gender was not a consideration in the selection. Of course, there are many brilliant female filmmakers at work today, from Agnès Varda and Claire Denis in France to Jane Campion in Australia and Kathryn Bigelow in the US et al. Certain of these were approached to take part, but ultimately they were unavailable.

There are many people to thank in the assembly of this volume, starting with my talented and patient editors at Ilex Press, Natalia Price-Cabrera and Zara Larcombe.

Thanks also to Sen-lun Yu, who conducted the Zhang Yimou interview in person in Beijing and translated it from Mandarin to English, and Ian Sandwell for his tireless transcription; Barbara Peira Aso and Liliana Niespial at El Deseo; Sylvie Barthet; Sara Chloe Cantor; Zeynep Ozbatur and Azize Tan; Tania Antonioli and Delphine Tomson at Les Films du Fleuve; Magali Montet, Alya Belgaroui and Franck Garbarz, who acted as a translator when I spoke to the Dardennes; Gary Unger at Exile Entertainment; the wonderful Maureen O'Malley at Warner Bros International; Jenne Casarotto, Cate Kane and Linda Drew; Amy Lord; Martin Schweighofer who graciously translated for me in our meeting with Michael Haneke, Roland Fischer-Briand and Alexander Horwath at the Austrian Film Museum; Wonjo Jeong for his brilliant translation of Park Chan-wook, and Se Young Kang and Jean Noh; Kerry Dibbs, Kirsty Langdale and Matthew Hampton. Finally, a very big thank you, as always, to Christopher Rowley.

Mike Goodridge

Pedro Almodóvar

"When you are a director you have to have your own language, you have to be in possession of that language and the vision of the story you want to tell through the film you are making."

Born in 1949, Pedro Almodóvar started making films in the immediate aftermath of the fall of Franco, and his irreverent, sexually adventurous melodramas represented the new wave of bold, culturally relevant cinema in Spain and indeed the rest of the world. Since the 1980s, his raw, vital and colorful cinema has developed a global following, losing some of its edge, as Almodóvar grew older and gaining in its place a sophistication and maturity that has almost made him respectable.

He is the most celebrated Spanish filmmaker of a generation and one of the most beloved in the world, one of the few to spawn his own adjective "Almodóvarian."

Influenced by classic Hollywood cinema, as well as Buñuel, Fassbinder and Fellini, he made his first film **Pepi, Luci, Bom and Other Girls Like Mom** (1980) on an ultra-low budget, but it teamed him for the first time with actress Carmen Maura, establishing a series of partnerships with actors that would include Antonio Banderas, Cecilia Roth, Marisa Paredes, Chus Lampreave, Rossy de Palma, Victoria Abril, and most recently Penélope Cruz. His earlier films, including **Matador** (1986) and **Law of Desire** (1987), built him a cult reputation throughout the world, but it was his delirious screwball comedy, **Women on the Verge of a Nervous Breakdown** in 1988, which brought him mainstream fame and his first Oscar nomination. Through the 1990s he made hits such as **Tie Me Up! Tie Me Down!** (1990), **High Heels** (1991), **The Flower of My Secret** (1995), and **Live Flesh** (1997), cementing his reputation as an iconic filmmaker.

With his gloriously emotional **All About My Mother** in 1999, he entered a new era of acceptance, winning the Oscar and the best director award at Cannes. His 2002 follow-up **Talk to Her** was even more acclaimed, winning him a second Oscar for best original screenplay and a nomination for best director—rare for a foreign-language filmmaker. His biggest ever commercial hit **Volver** came in 2006, winning Cruz an Oscar nomination and a prize for best actress at Cannes, shared with the other lead actresses in the film.

His most recent film, **The Skin I Live In** (2011), reunited him with Banderas for the first time in twenty-one years.

Pedro Almodóvar

" It's very difficult to explain the origins of everything in a film because it's very mysterious and many things happen by chance. You have to be writing all the time and in my case I make notes all the time. I am always working on four or five ideas and there comes a time when I decide to just write one.

You never ever really feel that you are going to be able to pull off the project that you are working on. You never have complete confidence. But of course there comes a time when you feel that you have learnt the trade and the craft of making films, so I feel now that I know the language and how to use it to get a particular emotion. But even if you know all the elements of the technique, you need something else. You need vision, a lot of honesty, strong imagination, and control of that imagination. Language is something quite easy to learn, but the most important thing in a film is your point of view, your vision, and how you look at the world around you.

You never feel absolutely sure about the final outcome because all the different components that make up the film are alive as you make it. One of those elements, of course, is the people. In a film you've got forty, fifty or sixty people working with you and the most difficult thing is controlling them, not because they are trying to rebel against you or not obeying you, but because the material you are using to make the film is alive and they are interacting with it as well. So sometimes the end result is not the one you are looking for. The stamp or style you put on your films is extremely personal and there really aren't that many rules governing it, because what might work for Orson Welles or for David Lynch doesn't necessarily work for me at all. So you have to seek out your own preferences, the way you would like to use language, and it's something you just get over time, little by little. I still haven't discovered it fully yet. I am still working on it.

I remember that all through the 1980s, I was developing my own filmmaking style with a very specific aesthetic stamp on it. So in the late eighties, from **Women on the Verge of a Nervous Breakdown**, everything the people in the décor department brought me was over the top. It was almost too Almodóvar-y which is exactly what I didn't want. It was almost as if the Almodóvar style had become a cliché.

I battle against cliché. If you give a dramatic role to an actor who is suffering in their personal life, it is very easy for that actor or actress to cry. But I don't want those real tears. For me the movie is always a representation of reality in every sense, from the actors to the lighting. I want their tears to be artificial as well.

When you're a director you have to have your own language, you have to be in possession of that language and the vision of the story you want to tell through the film you are making. On top of that you also have to have bags of common sense and be very strong because you are a boss in the best and worst sense, and you have to demonstrate this all the time. You have to make 100 decisions every moment.

When you're shooting a film—and this is something François Truffaut said—it's like a runaway train. The brakes have failed and the director's job is to ensure that that train doesn't go off the rails at all. Some directors, even though they're extremely talented as filmmakers, just

01 María Barranco, Rossy de Palma, and Antonio Banderas in **Women on the Verge of a Nervous Breakdown**

don't have the resilience to be able to cope with that process. And I really think that there are too many directors around who have that authority to be able to cope with the filmmaking and too few really talented ones who haven't been able to last. Because you have to deal with the human factor and that human factor can destroy you.

I remember when I was making **Dark Habits** (1983), there was one actress who was playing her first leading role, and as the days of shooting went on, I realized she wasn't up to what the role demanded of her. So what I did was pass a lot of the dialogue on to actresses who were playing the roles of the nuns. I stripped her of the things she was supposed to be doing and during production that all went into the community of nuns in the film. Their roles got richer and richer. When you are shooting you discover things like this that you cannot discover during rehearsals; because in rehearsals you don't have the props or the action.

How do I control all these elements? I repeat myself to the crew over and over again. If I want a specific blue color on the wall, I get them to paint the whole spectrum of blues from gray to blue and then I point out exactly which one I want. It's almost like being a painter gathering materials, but this time in three dimensions.

If I want to set up the scene with a table and two chairs and an armchair, I already have an idea in my mind of the colors, the composition,

and the form of it all, so what I do is give photos to the design team to go off and find it for me. They bring me examples of the different tables and I try them out. It's all through trial and error, moving things around, changing their position and checking what works together.

This process makes my filmmaking more painstaking than it could otherwise be, but I must also work in this way with my actors. It takes an awful long time to get the hairstyles right or the way they will dress. I take a long time trying things out with the actors because they never →

02–04 Almodóvar's biggest commercial hit thus far, **Volver**, starring Penélope Cruz and Carmen Maura

ALL ABOUT MY MOTHER

(01–05) Classic movies often play a central role in Almodóvar's films. "The little snippets of films you see in my films are not just about paying tribute to another film or director," says Almodóvar, "they are actually part of the narrative, and form a meaning as part of the plot."

In the opening moments of **All About My Mother**, Manuela (Cecilia Roth) is watching **All About Eve** with her son **(01)**. "The scene they are watching takes place in a dressing room **(02)** and for me the dressing room is like the holy sanctuary of females," he says. "It reminds me of the patios or courtyards of the houses where I used to live. So what I am saying in this sequence is that this is all about women, lots of different types of women. Margo Channing is an actress, Eve Harrington wants to be an actress and is a fanatic about the theater. The scene is like a summing up of all the important things that will come up in my film. I like to set out the main themes straight away in the first sequence of any film I am making."

"Then the mother and son go off to see **A Streetcar Named Desire (03)** and the son ends up dying waiting to ask for an autograph from one of the actresses. It's almost like he has been run down by the very streetcar of desire. He has just plucked up the courage to ask his mother who his father is and the only thing she will say is that when he was conceived, she and his father were actors playing Stanley and Stella in an amateur production of the play. So it's a little like they are rehearsing something that's going to happen in the future in real life. **All About Eve** and **A Streetcar Named Desire** are the two pillars underpinning the whole narrative structure of the film."

TALK TO HER

(06–07) Almodóvar says that he is always sincere in his stories, however outrageous they might appear, and he never judges his characters. In his 2002 classic **Talk to Her**, for example, his lead character Benigno, a nurse, rapes a woman in his care who is in a coma.

"The origin of that was something I read that had happened in New York—that an orderly in a hospital had raped a girl in a coma and that she became pregnant. I was so shocked that someone in that state could create life. So I started writing **Talk to Her**, but I cannot—and this is something I discovered throughout my career— write about a character if I don't feel a kind of empathy for them. So I tried to explain this nurse who could commit this crime, his human condition, his humanity, how he is living. This is the challenge for me and this is very appealing because sometimes you have to explain to the audience how a character can arrive at this situation. From the moment you understand Benigno, then you too can feel empathy for him and accept that he commits this crime. I was scared when I made the film because I didn't know what people were going to think, especially in America, where political correctness is like a dictatorship. This film is the opposite and I was always very incorrect politically. Curiously, and fortunately, it was rather well received in America."

feel they are in character until they know what the character looks like. Just simple decisions like the length of hair that an actress should have take ages to work out. I come along with lots of fashion and hair magazines, and photos of ideas that I have with exactly the length of the hair the actress should have, but everyone's hair is different, so you still have to see if it works with their hair.

For instance, it took ages to get that very natural, unhairdo-like style that Penélope had in **Volver**. It was supposed to look like she had just put it up, but the amount of time it took you would think we had constructed some elaborate hairdo. But it worked and was incredible. What is important is not to give up on the small things.

Of course, **Volver** had a strong relation to Italian neorealism, and, unlike the women in

Spanish neorealist films, the women are very attractive. So I saw in my mind that I wanted a very attractive look. Then you have to take into account the social class of the character and how women from that class would look and you have to add a touch of humor. I did lots of research going into the homes of that type of housewife from that social class and picking out the little, funny details that I could replicate in the film. There are all sorts of color schemes you see in these homes, but by that point I had already made up my mind of exactly the range of colors I would be working with. I always do that through intuition when I finish a script and just before I start shooting. I have already made up my mind about the spectrum of colors in the film that I will be making. Before all this I always have a very →

THE SKIN I LIVE IN

(01–09) Almodóvar explains how he visualized the settings and design for the house and its interiors in **The Skin I Live In**. Most of the film's action takes place in the discreet luxury house owned by the megalomaniacal surgeon Dr. Robert Ledgard (as played by Antonio Banderas) and which houses his housekeeper Marilia (Marisa Paredes) and his prisoner, the mysterious Vera (Elena Anaya).

"The story needed a house that it is not easy to see from the outside," he explains. "So the house I was looking for in my mind was a country house close to a big town or city, but it had to be almost like a natural, closed prison. We found this big country house just 4km away from the city of Toledo that has three sets of locked gateways to get into, and which you can't see into from the outside. If you are not invited in, nobody will open the gate for you. This is the house where the three characters live and the very first thing I had to do to make the film was find this location."

(01–04) Almodóvar asked designer Juan Gatti to create pictures based on 100-year-old natural-science books that would reflect the film's theme of transgenesis. "You see them in the doctor's office on the wall behind his desk (01)," he says. The figure of the man was also used as the poster for the film (02).

Using detail to add to the narrative

(05–09) Almodóvar added visual ideas to the setting in **The Skin I Live In**, which illustrate how small details and decoration deepen what's happening on screen.

A large rug in the entrance hall of the house was created for the film based on an abstract painting by Ben Nicholson (07). "I wanted Vera's character to be caught there, trapped in an abstract painting," Almodóvar says. "It was quite risky, but I love the painting and I wanted it to become a big rug. It's an intuition I have and I take those kinds of risks all the time. When Vera is threatening the doctor with a knife, she is standing on the rug and trapped in that abstraction."

(08) Vera's room was painted in a range of grays and light browns to illustrate Almodóvar's idea that the room would be "as uniform as possible and those are the most neutral colors. There were as few accessories and pieces of furniture as possible to accentuate that sameness."

However, at the center of the room, is the bed in a bold red that stands out from the neutral color scheme. "Her room is a prison cell so my real aim was to have it as antiseptic an environment as possible, but the red breaks that apart and red is the key color I use to have that impact." Almodóvar also looked to great artworks from the past for inspiration, for example, Titian's *Venus of Urbino* (09). And designer Juan Gatti created two original works especially for use in the film (05–06).

clear idea of the whole narrative process itself as the film goes on. For me writing and directing are symbiotic, complementary. While I am writing, I am working out the moments when you are giving information to the audiences, and the moments when you are withholding information. How that works is the narrative flow through the film, the way the characters are built up, and how they react or interact with each other. This is all very clear in my mind when I am writing the script. The script also includes the atmosphere I want to feature in each scene, and the songs that each have a dramatic function and are integral to the script.

The importance of arts in general in my films can't be underestimated. When I am writing the script, I am always going out because everything you see, everything you hear, every movie you see, you watch it and it informs the sensibility of the story you are writing. So I was writing **The Skin I Live In** when I saw an exhibition of Louise Bourgeois at the Tate Modern, and Vera is looking at a book of her work in the film. It is a way for her to survive.

Songs are also very important. Cucurrucucú Paloma is a very famous Mexican song and there have been thousands of versions, but when I heard the Caetano Veloso version, I was amazed because the song became something completely different. It became a dark lullaby, very moving. Then in **Talk to Her**, I present the character of Marco as a man who cries at certain times, so I needed a song to play in the party scene that was moving enough to make him cry. This is very risky because there is no way for the production to declare that at 1 am we will have deep emotion. But I needed that emotion because otherwise the audience wouldn't understand that this was a man who cried with emotion. Then I tried to think of things that really move me a lot and one of those things was Caetano's song, so I called him and asked him to perform it in the film. I was right because he was amazing and the situation is intriguing.

Likewise, a song gives **Volver** its title. **Volver** is all about this great Spanish tradition of the dead

coming back to settle unsettled accounts. So **Volver** is coming back from beyond.

Sometimes I have things in my mind that aren't visible in the final film, but they are important for me because they give me a basis from which I can jumpstart the story. I had a whole back story in my mind for Penélope's character in **Volver**— she was a beautiful young girl who her mother adored, and she wanted her to be a singer and a performer and taught her this song "Volver" so she could go and perform it in auditions for little girls—which is exactly the same story you see in **Bellissima** [the Visconti classic featuring Anna Magnani in the mother role]. There's a part in the film in the kitchen where Carmen Maura says to Penélope, "Did you always have big boobs like that?" and she says, "Yes, mummy, ever since I was a little girl." So for the auditions, the mother puts makeup on her and puts her in amazing dresses. Her father sees all this and it must have been quite a vision for him, so much so that he couldn't resist the temptation. There was always a lot of incest within the family in these households in La Mancha.

So when Penélope sings the song that her mother taught her in the film, she is remembering her mother very tenderly, even though she thought the mother didn't do anything about the father raping her. And it is very moving for the mother, who is listening from the car on the street, because the song is talking about the

01 Almodóvar filming Penélope Cruz in **Broken Embraces** (2009)

02 Antonio Banderas in **Law of Desire**

03 Dark Habits

04 Almodóvar on set

Advice to young filmmakers

"The hope lies with young filmmakers because they are the ones least bound to anyone in the industry. They are the least caught up in success and don't have to think about the market and what's going to be successful. When I started out back in the 1980s, it was a very special time in Spain, we had this flourishing blossom of freedom, and people in fashion and painting and filmmaking were doing it out of the sheer pleasure and joy of being able to do it. We never thought about the market or whether there was a market. That's the problem today: the market is everything and there is far more competition. But if you are starting, that really is the moment. Your film might be seen by five people, but that doesn't matter. You are not bound to anyone, the industry or the financier or the studio. Our young filmmakers are the ones who can make exciting, groundbreaking films because they only need low budgets and it's much cheaper to get the team. A 25-year-old is definitely someone more likely to take risks than a veteran film director who's got two homes and a family, and needs to make sure his film makes money. So, to young filmmakers I say, don't have any preconceived ideas about what you're doing. Don't try to be old or modern. Just be true to yourself when you are making your films. You are not bound by anybody."

passing of time. It is almost like the daughter is sending an unconscious message to her mother that she doesn't really hate her, despite the passing of time.

   None of that is actually explained in the film at all, but my movies are all about secrets and the secret intentions I have that give me the reason to work. Of course, they are not visible, but the audience can feel that strength. „

Advice to young filmmakers

"The hope lies with young filmmakers because they are the ones least bound to anyone in the industry. They are the least caught up in success and don't have to think about the market and what's going to be successful. When I started out back in the 1980s, it was a very special time in Spain, we had this flourishing blossom of freedom, and people in fashion and painting and filmmaking were doing it out of the sheer pleasure and joy of being able to do it. We never thought about the market or whether there was a market. That's the problem today: the market is everything and there is far more competition. But if you are starting, that really is the moment. Your film might be seen by five people, but that doesn't matter. You are not bound to anyone, the industry or the financier or the studio. Our young filmmakers are the ones who can make exciting, groundbreaking films because they only need low budgets and it's much cheaper to get the team. A 25-year-old is definitely someone more likely to take risks than a veteran film director who's got two homes and a family, and needs to make sure his film makes money. So, to young filmmakers I say, don't have any preconceived ideas about what you're doing. Don't try to be old or modern. Just be true to yourself when you are making your films. You are not bound by anybody."

passing of time. It is almost like the daughter is sending an unconscious message to her mother that she doesn't really hate her, despite the passing of time.

   None of that is actually explained in the film at all, but my movies are all about secrets and the secret intentions I have that give me the reason to work. Of course, they are not visible, but the audience can feel that strength. „

Olivier Assayas

"I design my shots very precisely. I use floor plans of the set and just design the evolutions of the camera and the respective positions of the actors. That's the kind of security I need when I get on set in the morning."

The son of French screenwriter and filmmaker Jacques Rémy, Olivier Assayas made shorts and wrote for French cinephile publication **Cahiers du Cinéma** before making his feature film debut in 1986 with psychological drama **Désordre (Disorder)**. A string of well-received character pieces followed—**Winter's Child** (1989), **Paris s'éveille (Paris Awakens**, 1991), **A New Life** (1993) and, in particular, **L'eau froide (Cold Water**, 1994) starring Virginie Ledoyen, which was selected for Un Certain Regard at the Cannes Film Festival. However, Assayas started to explore outside France with **Irma Vep** in 1996, a playful take on Louis Feuillade's silent serial **Les Vampires (Irma Vep** is an anagram of "Vampire").

This film, combined with his 1998 documentary **HHH: A Portrait of Hou Hsiao Hsien**, showed his passion for Asian cinema. He went back to France for his next two films—**Late August, Early September** (1998), and a lavish period piece **Les destinées sentimentales** (2000)—but returned to international territory in 2002 with his first English-language film **Demonlover**, a technological thriller starring Connie Nielsen and Chloë Sevigny. From then on, his career has stepped in and out of France. His 2004 drama **Clean**, set in Canada and Paris, won Maggie Cheung the best actress award at Cannes for her portrayal of a junkie trying to clean up her act. His 2007 gangster thriller **Boarding Gate** featured Asia Argento, and takes place in both Paris and Hong Kong.

He received the best reviews in his career to date for **L'heure d'été (Summer Hours**, 2008). Then, changing gear again in 2010, he delivered his mightiest accomplishment to date—**Carlos**—a riveting 330-minute epic about the rise and fall of Venezuelan terrorist Carlos The Jackal, who wreaked havoc across Europe throughout the 1970s. Featuring a star-making performance by Édgar Ramírez, and told in multiple languages, the film—which also screened as a TV mini-series across the world—was the sensation of the 2010 Cannes Film Festival, and won a Golden Globe for best mini-series of the year and multiple critical acclaim.

In typical Assayas fashion, he subsequently retreated to a small semi-autobiographical drama about a Paris teenager in the early 1970s called **Something in the Air** (2012).

Olivier Assayas

"I am not a film-critic-turned-filmmaker. I have always wanted to make films and I started by making short films, but I was unhappy with the short films and felt that I was not mature enough to make a feature. Somehow, writing for *Cahiers du Cinéma* in Paris was an opportunity to structure my approach to cinema, to understand my place in film history and make sense of what I would go on to do as a filmmaker.

Cahiers du Cinéma was a school of international cinema for me because it allowed me to travel to film festivals, where I was exposed to movies from all over the world, movies that I would not be able to see at home. I went to Asia, to the US, I learned about the international geopolitics of cinema, and that is what defined my approach to the medium.

French cinema can be very insular. In France, as an independent filmmaker, you don't have to put your nose outside the window and to me it is extremely frustrating. My first film, **Désordre**, takes place in Paris, Brighton, London and New York, so there was a notion of travel in it, but then I went back to functioning within the framework of French independent cinema and, as happy as I am with the movies I made at that time, I felt my vision of the world was restricted. France limited the tools I had at my disposal to describe the modern world. That has to do with the French language, of course, and English happens to be the international language, so I knew that at some point I wanted to deal with that. Over time I started to become much less shy in my use of foreign languages and it took me all the way to **Carlos** where the characters speak every language in the world.

Making a first feature is about having the maturity to understand that the movie is not about pyrotechnics or thrills, it's about looking at your actors, and I knew that I had to start by getting good performances from my actors. The reason I can't even watch the short films I made is because the acting is disastrous. The camera is cool and the movies look cool, so if you turn off the sound, they look interesting, but if you turn on the sound and listen to the acting, it's like a seven-year-old trying to play the violin.

When you are young and you want to be a filmmaker, you have zero training in terms of functioning with actors. When you work for the stage, it's your everyday job to direct actors, so you figure things out if it's naïve or clumsy. I had no idea how to direct my actors; in the shorts I wasn't even writing things for them to play. I had to work out my own way of functioning with actors, so I could get genuine performances out of them and I kind of made it in **Désordre** and tried to grow from there.

Working with a very important French filmmaker, André Téchiné, for whom I wrote **Rendez-vous** (1985) and **Scene of the Crime** (1986), made me understand how to write for actors. Once you thought about the scenes in terms of feelings and emotions that were to be expressed in their own way by your actors, you had taken a major step.

When I am writing, the only thing I have to be confident with is the skeleton. I start writing when I feel that there is a logic to the chain of events, that it has a skeleton that I can build around. I have to know that it has its own dramatic logic. I can play around with it, but ultimately I always know where I am coming from and where I am going. It's a complete chain of implications and consequences.

01 **Clean**, set in both Canada and Paris, won Maggie Cheung the best actress award at Cannes for her portrayal of a junkie trying to clean up her act

> "I learnt a lot for **Carlos** when I was making **Les destinées sentimentales**. I learned how that, even with a bigger-than-usual budget, you end up struggling because you never have enough money to make a film. And I learned how to work really fast and make a film very sharply."

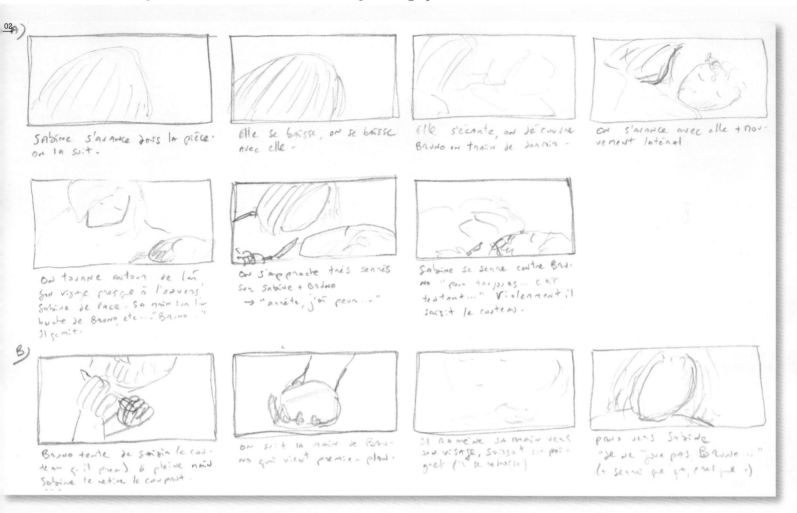

I am a very precise writer and, in the same way, I design my shots very precisely. I use floor plans of the set and just design the evolutions of the camera and the respective positions of the actors. That's the kind of security I need when I get on set in the morning.

With actors, I just need to have a sense that they have absorbed the lines and made them their own, so when I start hearing dialogue exactly as I have written it, I get nervous that they are not absorbing it and appropriating it. Often, I go to the actor and change lines on the spot, so he has no time to absorb the exact line, but gets the idea. I constantly change the dialogue so that the actors are not dependent on something they

have rehearsed or anticipated. And I am always waiting and hoping for their own ideas. Édgar Ramírez is an extremely creative actor, so is Maggie Cheung. I think neither of them in their home industries had been given that freedom, Édgar in Hollywood or Venezuela, Maggie in Hong Kong, so when you suddenly open the door for them, they just rush in.

I've been working with the same core group of collaborators ever since I started. The set designer of **Carlos** was the set designer of my first film. One of the two cameramen of **Carlos**, Denis Lenoir, was also on **Désordre**. Likewise Luc Barnier, who edited **Carlos**, was on **Désordre**. I have been working with my →

02 Assayas often incorporates his own hand-drawn storyboards into the writing process. The example shown here is from **Winter's Child**

CARLOS

(01–04) Remarkably, **Carlos** cost just 13 million Euros to produce. Assayas shot for 92 days in France, Germany, Austria, Hungary, the UK, Lebanon, Morocco, Sudan, and Yemen. Although shot in 35mm and in widescreen format, it was financed principally by French pay-TV giant CANAL+. "I see it as a movie that basically cannot be financed within the framework of cinema because it's too long, had no famous actors and was spoken in every single possible language," says Assayas. "I had to use TV money because if I went to a film producer and told him I wanted to do a five-and-a-half-hour movie about a famous terrorist who is the most hated person in France starring a new actor from Venezuela, he would have had me arrested. Whereas if I go to a TV channel, they might think that they could do it in three parts and it would be interesting. What is wildly crazy in one medium is normal in another."

(01) "We shot a huge amount of footage each day," he adds. "There were so many scenes, so many characters, so many transformations because time passes in the story and in the same two-day period, the same character would have to play at three different ages with makeup or prosthetics."

Assayas said the shoot was "long if you compare it to one film and extremely short if you compare it to three. We never had enough time. The whole thing was monstrously long and because we had to make two different versions [a three-hour theatrical film was also cut in addition to the 330-minute total version], it was very complicated."

01 A page from the script with photos of the location alongside showing a crucial action sequence from **Carlos**

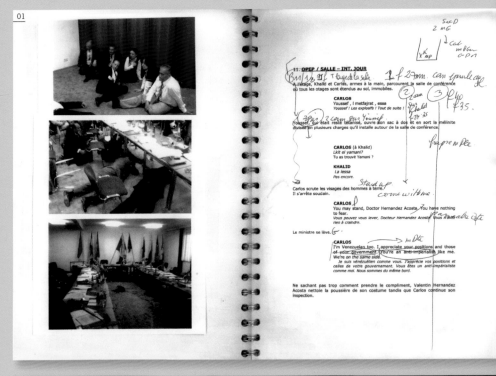

Chaos and filmmaking

Carlos also represented a watershed moment in Assayas' technique of blending precise preparation with spontaneity and improvisation. "What I understood through the years and from movie to movie is that you need to have the space in every single shot for improvisation. You know exactly what your shot will be, what will happen in the shot and what the characters will say, but there has to be room for your actors to bring their own words, instinct and intuition to the scene. I was lucky on **Carlos** to have actors who grabbed that opportunity, to enhance whatever initial material we had. We never rehearsed, not even technically. I hate rehearsing usually. I never do readings before a shoot. I do my best to preserve the spontaneity of the first day, but even if you function that way, you usually do technical rehearsals just to make sure everyone understands the position of the camera or whether it's longer, dolly or handheld shots."

"But on **Carlos**, I would trust the chaos," he continues. "Chaos is the filmmaker's best ally. I would get on the set and describe the shots to the cameraman, to the grip, the soundman and the actors. It was probably a real-life event and I would describe the shot very precisely, but in the back of my mind I knew they wouldn't be able to absorb the whole thing and they would have to adapt. So the crew had to be extremely aware and tense because everything was ultimately fluid."

ÉDGAR RAMÍREZ AS CARLOS

(02–04) For the pivotal role of Carlos, Assayas cast Édgar Ramírez, a Venezuelan actor who had made a name for himself in Hollywood movies like **Domino** (2005) and **The Bourne Ultimatum** (2007). "Édgar is a brilliant actor," says Assayas. "He is inventive, resourceful, warm, and generous." Ramírez flew to Paris from Colombia, where he was shooting, to meet with Assayas for the role. "He understood the politics of those years, he spoke the languages and I instantly learned things about Carlos from him because he's from that culture. I had never been to Venezuela, so it was enlightening to hear him speak, hear how he reacted and realize that his kind of energy and physicality is something not European. When we had dinner the first time we met, I understood that if you put a guy like that in the middle of leftist intellectual Europeans, he would be a completely different breed. It was not something that I had to imagine, that I would somehow have to build the character around the actor," he continues. "It's something that he radiated, that just came from him and it's only once in a while that that happens."

"Sometimes everything went wrong and you just threw the first take away. Sometimes it all fell into place in extremely interesting ways. The thing is that you instantly know what works and what does not work in the take, so instead of trying to solve every single technical problem, we just jumped in, and by the second take everyone knew what was going on. This process allowed us to do very complex things extremely fast with a certain degree of liberty for the actors, because I never ever want to see a mark on the ground. I used marks in my early films and it was a nightmare to tell the actor their positions. Every time I see a mark taped on the floor, I go wild."

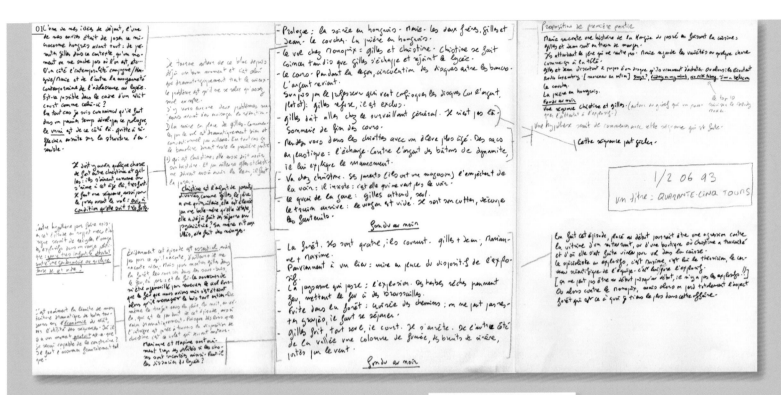

L'EAU FROIDE

(01–02) This was Assayas' first film to play at Cannes and was the story of a bunch of listless young people in Paris and outside. (02) Pictured are Polaroid samples of the casting featuring the film's lead actress, Virginie Ledoyen (the Polaroid with the blue dot on it). The notes page shows how Assayas constructed the narrative and psychology of the script in chunks of connecting notes (01).

producer, Sylvie Barthet, since 1994. There has been a very solid continuity.

These collaborations are incredibly helpful because I always have a feeling that I made my movies with budgets that were too small. It's always about putting much more on screen than the money we actually have, so you have to come up with creative solutions constantly, and if you have people who are used to your way of working and who have that kind of problem-solving culture, they become integral to your filmmaking. I have only ever worked with three cameramen—Denis Lenoir, Eric Gautier, and Yorick Le Saux—and when they are not available, I'm kind of stuck. There are very few cinematographers who understand the way I shoot, who work in the middle ground between very precisely designed shots and improvisation. I also love to work extremely fast. It's a high-wire

act really and only works on my movies because of the common, shared experience.

Different cameramen bring different elements. When I am working with Yorick, he is such an easygoing, fast, adaptable guy that I know I can try crazy things with him because it's never too late or dark. Everything is possible. Denis is a little bit like that but a little bit less, so once in a while he stops the process and asks for five minutes to light the set because otherwise it would look mad. Eric will slow me down in the right moments. He will say, we can't do this shot today because the light is wrong, let's do it tomorrow when we will have some sun. He worked miracles on **Summer Hours**, because during the whole shoot we must have had a total of twelve hours of sunshine, and during those scattered twelve hours we managed to get all the sunshine we needed. That was thanks to him. I would never have had the patience.

In my films, you see the movement and the energy in the camerawork. It's something to do with the relationship between cinema and painting. Some filmmakers imagine that the relationship is with the framing. Actually, because I've been a painter myself, I believe it's with the brush stroke. So I work in visible brush strokes. It's kinetic and has its own musicality. The music is in the mixture of camera movement and cutting.

The way I work now is that I make different versions of every single shot, in the sense that from one take to the other, the shot is evolving. The first take will be more or less what I had in mind and just watching it, I will have another idea and will change it. After a while, when we get to the tenth take, it's completely different to what we were doing in the first take.

But then I know that, even if I end up using the tenth take, there is something in the first and second takes that I can also use. Basically, what I am saying is that I try to capture through the camera some unique moments and ultimately a lot of my movies are made up of tiny unique moments that only exist within one specific take. I often edit fairly quickly because I don't have much choice as a specific moment, a specific expression only happened once and was not even planned, but invariably came out of the evolution of the shot.

One of the disturbing elements of filmmaking is that you have a completely different eye when you are editing, meaning that I would remember that on a particular scene we did a really good fourth take, but then when I look at the fourth take in editing I don't understand why I liked it so much. My focus has completely changed and one of the takes that I hardly noticed ends up being the most graceful and precise.

I am more objective when I am editing, I am outside the logistics of the film. When I am on set, I can't protect myself from the logistics, from what's going on. When I am editing, I am in the narration and am concerned only with what makes sense in terms of the previous shot and the next one.

I love editing. I am there every day. The editor doesn't touch the film when I'm not there. I'm not there just to look over the shoulder of the editor, I'm there because I love it. It's one of the most exciting moments in cinema. I love to edit fast, to capture scenes really sharply. Then again, sometimes Luc Barnier [Assayas' editor] is the guy who just wants to speed things up and I slow him down, and other times, it's the opposite. We have a really interesting dynamic between us.

The one thing that took me the most time to understand in the process of filmmaking, and ultimately the most valuable, is that to focus on the emotions I am experiencing and make sure they are in the film. When you are on location, you can have a sense of space or experience some moment of beauty—sunshine, rain—and I insist that everything that comes to me in the process of shooting has to be absorbed by the film. In my earlier films, I was too concerned with control and didn't want to be distracted by the beauty of the landscape.

In every single film, there are always moments when you are shooting that you look at an actor speaking dialogue and the thing takes on a life of its own. It has its own life. That's the moment you understand that the movie is working. You know you have hit the right chord for that specific film. It always happens. I remember when we were shooting **Irma Vep**, there was a moment when Nathalie Richard, who was playing a costume designer, goes to Bulle Ogier and tells her that →

03 Assayas with actors Juliette Binoche and Kyle Eastwood on the set of **Summer Hours**, an elegiac family drama set between a sleepy country house and the frenetic pace of Paris. It is one of Assayas' most acclaimed films and was named best foreign-language film by a host of US critics groups

IRMA VEP

(01–03) During a three-month period when his big-budget French period piece **Les destinées sentimentales** was delayed, Assayas spent nine days writing what he calls his "crazy kamikaze movie" **Irma Vep**. "I found some money for it and we shot it in four weeks," he says. "It's a movie which uses a lot of elements that I had never dared use in my filmmaking before, meaning a mixture of French and English, using Hong Kong pop culture, using film clips, and dealing in an ironic way with the film theory of the time."

Central to **Irma Vep** was Maggie Cheung [who would become Assayas' wife], the iconic Hong Kong film star **(01–02)**. He first met her at Venice International Film Festival in 1995 where he was on the jury and watched her in Wong Kar-wai's **Ashes of Time** (1994). "I was absolutely struck by the fact that she was a movie star," he says. "I was not sure that the notion of movie star meant anything to me in terms of my filmmaking. I had never worked with any. I had hardly worked with famous actors at all because it was against the texture of real-life genuine characters that I was looking for. And then when I saw Maggie, I thought, 'God, she has the specific glow of a movie star, but she is 100 percent modern and completely relevant.' So the question came to me, what would happen if I used someone in one of my films who comes from a completely different culture, who has a different way of acting, who has a completely different way of using her physicality, her body? She is an actress who does not exist in French film culture, so what happens if I bring someone alien to French film culture? It was like an experiment mixing chemicals and, of course, she glows in the film. It's probably the cheapest movie-star vehicle ever made." **(03)** The first page of Assayas' handwritten script for the film, which took only nine days to write.

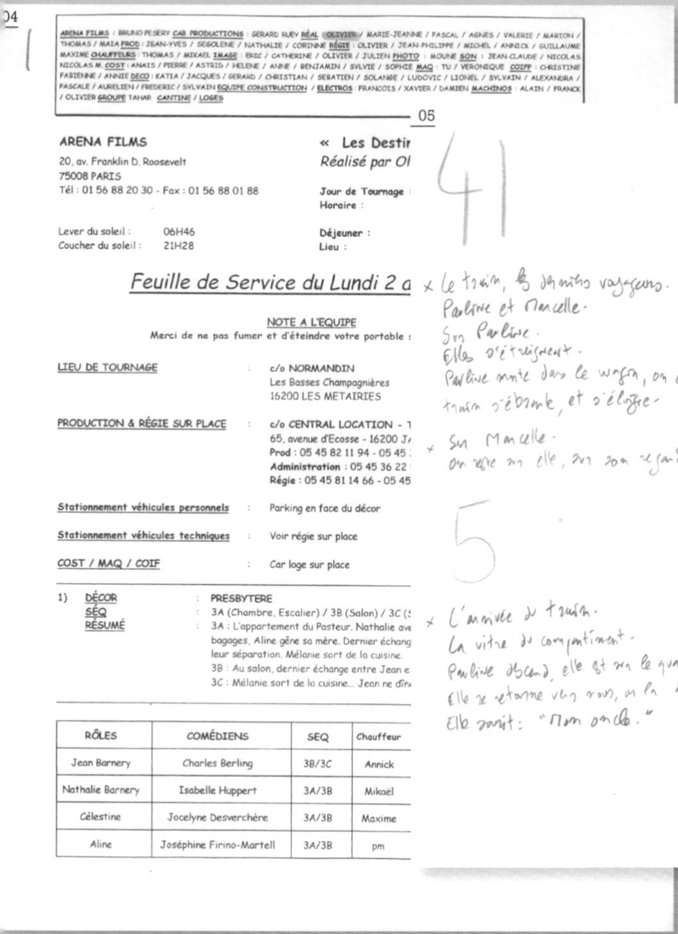

(04) ARENA FILMS | BRUNO PESERY CAB PRODUCTIONS / GERARD RUEY RÉAL / OLIVIER / MARIE-JEANNE / PASCAL / AGNES / VALERIE / MARION / THOMAS / MAIA PROD: JEAN-YVES / SEGOLENE / NATHALIE / CORINNE RÉGIE / OLIVIER / JEAN-PHILIPPE / MICHEL / ANNICK / GUILLAUME MAXIME CHAUFFEURS: THOMAS / MIKAEL IMAGE: ERIC / CATHERINE / OLIVIER / JULIEN PHOTO / MOUNE SON: JEAN-CLAUDE / NICOLAS NICOLAS M. COST: ANAIS / PIERRE / ASTRID / HELENE / ANNE / BENJAMIN / SYLVIE / SOPHIE MAQ: TU / VERONIQUE COIFF: CHRISTINE FABIENNE / ANNIE DÉCO: KATIA / JACQUES / GERARD / CHRISTIAN / SEBATIEN / SOLANGE / LUDOVIC / LIONEL / SYLVAIN / ALEXANDRA PASCALE / AURELIEN / FREDERIC / SYLVAIN ÉQUIPE CONSTRUCTION / ELECTROS: FRANCOIS / XAVIER / DAMIEN MACHINOS: ALAIN / FRANCK / OLIVIER GROUPE TAHAR CANTINE / LOGES

(05)

ARENA FILMS
20, av. Franklin D. Roosevelt
75008 PARIS
Tél : 01 56 88 20 30 - Fax : 01 56 88 01 88

« Les Destir
Réalisé par Ol

Jour de Tournage :
Horaire :

Lever du soleil :   06H46
Coucher du soleil : 21H28

Déjeuner :
Lieu :

Feuille de Service du Lundi 2 a

NOTE A L'EQUIPE
Merci de ne pas fumer et d'éteindre votre portable.

LIEU DE TOURNAGE	c/o NORMANDIN Les Basses Champagnières 16200 LES METAIRIES
PRODUCTION & RÉGIE SUR PLACE	c/o CENTRAL LOCATION - 1 65, avenue d'Ecosse - 16200 J/ Prod : 05 45 82 11 94 - 05 45 : Administration : 05 45 36 22 Régie : 05 45 81 14 66 - 05 45
Stationnement véhicules personnels	Parking en face du décor
Stationnement véhicules techniques	Voir régie sur place
COST / MAQ / COIF	Car loge sur place

1)	DÉCOR	: PRESBYTERE
	SÉQ	: 3A (Chambre, Escalier) / 3B (Salon) / 3C (S
	RÉSUMÉ	: 3A : L'appartement du Pasteur, Nathalie av bagages. Aline gêne sa mère. Dernier échang leur séparation. Mélanie sort de la cuisine. 3B : Au salon, dernier échange entre Jean e 3C : Mélanie sort de la cuisine... Jean e dîn

RÔLES	COMÉDIENS	SEQ	Chauffeur
Jean Barnery	Charles Berling	3B/3C	Annick
Nathalie Barnery	Isabelle Huppert	3A/3B	Mikaël
Célestine	Jocelyne Desverchère	3A/3B	Maxime
Aline	Joséphine Firino-Martell	3A/3B	pm

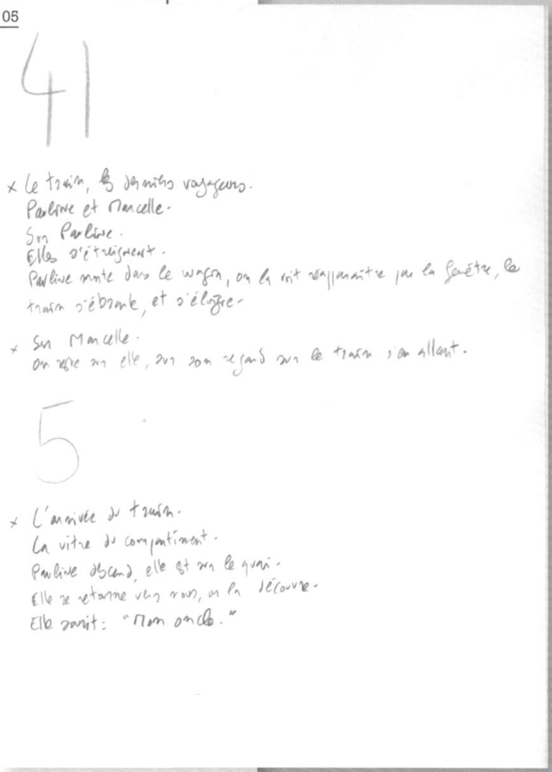

(handwritten notes)
41

x Le train, les derniers voyageurs.
Pauline et Marcelle.
Sur Pauline.
Elles s'étreignent.
Pauline monte dans le wagon, on la voit réapparaître par la fenêtre, le train s'ébranle, et s'éloigne.

x Sur Marcelle.
On revient sur elle, sur son regard sur le train s'en allant.

5

x L'arrivée du train.
La vitre du compartiment.
Pauline descend, elle est sur le quai.
Elle se retourne vers nous, on l'a découvre.
Elle sourit : "Mon oncle."

LES DESTINÉES SENTIMENTALES

(04–07) Assayas adapted **Les destinées sentimentales**, the novel by Jacques Chardonne, with Jacques Fieschi. It is his one nonoriginal movie, was made with a relatively big budget (around $15m), runs to three hours and featured big stars like Emmanuelle Béart **(06)**, Charles Berling **(07)**, and Isabelle Huppert.

"It was a very different process in that I had to get myself into the shoes of someone else for two years of my life. The novel is very autobiographical for Chardonne. It uses his own family background, his landscape, the places where he lived, the people that he knew, so I had to visit all those places, shoot in the actual places, or places closely resembling them, and call on his family members to become an expert on his work and life."

The story is set in Charente in the late 19th century and early 20th century, and encompasses both a Cognac distillery and a porcelain factory. "It meant I had to research an area of France I was not familiar with, understand the trade of Cognac in the early 20th century, understand how you create porcelain then and now, and so on. The whole thing was about absorbing the texture of someone's life and dealing with the past." **(04)** The first call sheet for the film. **(05)** A list of shots to be taken, handwritten by Assayas.

> "Assayas' two thrillers **Demonlover** and **Boarding Gate** were made, he explains, 'based on the faith that the thriller is the most experimental genre there is.'"

she is attracted to the Chinese actress. At that point Bulle Ogier goes to Maggie Cheung and tells her what Nathalie said. The way I wrote it was supposed to make people smile. We did the first take and Maggie blushed like she didn't know how to react. It brought a moment of unexpected trouble and gave truth to the situation beyond what I could have expected. The blush was something that came out of her that is way beyond the written word.

I don't have an Olivier Assayas style, really. I think I have a way of making films, of reacting to my actors or my material, but ultimately it's something that has to be adaptable to a variety of different perspectives of today's world. It's something I have been trying to adapt to different realities, including shooting in Hong Kong, or Japan, or Hungary. To me, movies are about exploring the world. **"**

Advice to young filmmakers

"Just look what's happening around you when you are shooting. No one really tells you that, but it's very important. Just don't think only of what's in your screenplay and what's useful for your story. Open your eyes to the world you are creating around you and eventually consider it might be more interesting or stronger than you had planned."

BOARDING GATE

(01–02) A key sequence in **Boarding Gate** takes place in the apartment of Michael Madsen's character Miles. The 24-minute sequence sees Sandra (Asia Argento) arrive at her ex-boyfriend Miles' two-story Paris apartment for a drink. The two reminisce about their sex-fueled past relationship, but the evening gets violent and it ends with Sandra shooting and killing Miles. In the sequence, the two actors move from living room to terrace to kitchen to bathroom, and Assayas' drawing **(02)** shows his plan for the scene along with a shot list. Argento is pictured on the terrace during the scene having removed her dress **(01)**.

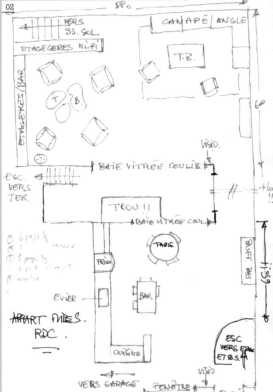

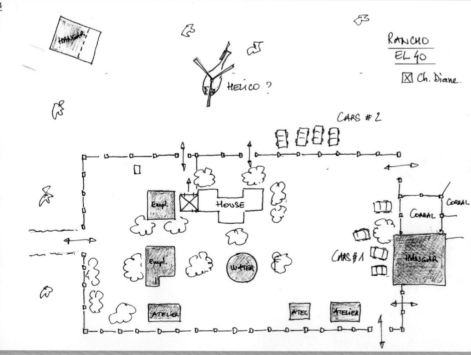

DEMONLOVER

(03–04) Demonlover follows various individuals and corporations vying over the control of the 3D anime pornography market; when an executive Diane (Connie Nielsen) discovers that one of the companies is a front for an interactive torture site, she is drawn into a vortex of intrigue and double crosses that will see her end up a torture victim of the site itself. The film takes place in Tokyo, Paris, the US and Mexico, and Diane's final incarceration is in a desert ranch in Mexico, from which she initially escapes. Assayas' drawing of the ranch compound shows the helicopter arrival pad as well as the room in which she is locked and from which she breaks out **(04)**. "The thriller is about this weird deal you have with the audience where if you give them the kind of thrills they want, in exchange you get away with experimenting with the form and the syntax. That is something, of course, which Hitchcock was a master of. He invented the concept. So what is interesting with genre filmmaking is that it's something that has got to be constantly redefined and, to me, making the thrillers was about reinventing. Thrillers are defined by visible and invisible forces, by conscious and subconscious forces, and you can deal with darker forces in them. For me it was the genre that helped me deal with issues that don't fit into more straightforward movies. In **Demonlover**, for example, it was about dealing with radically contemporary forces within modern society."

Susanne Bier

"As a director I have to be terrified of the material, and on a good percentage of shooting days I need to be terrified about how I am going to get the scene to where it needs to go."

Susanne Bier has become one of Denmark's most celebrated filmmakers, specializing in intense human melodramas so powerfully realized that they leave audiences breathless. Born in Copenhagen, she studied Art and Architecture at Jerusalem University before attending the National Film School Of Denmark, graduating in 1987. She made her debut feature **Freud Leaving Home** in 1991, and the first decade of her career was devoted to a series of commercial Danish and Swedish films. The film that kick-started her career into a different stratosphere was **The One and Only** (1999), which was the biggest Danish film of all time at the box office and won Denmark's Bodil Award for best film.

Bier achieved international recognition in 2002 when she signed on to direct a film made under the strict Dogme 95 filmmaking manifesto established by Lars von Trier. Written by Anders Thomas Jensen, **Open Hearts** (2002) tells the story of two couples thrown into a storm of anguish after a horrifying car accident. Its hyperrealistic treatment of a melodramatic premise would define the next phase in Bier's career, and highlighted her ability to coax extraordinary performances from her actors—in this case Mads Mikkelsen, Paprika Steen, and Nikolaj Lie Kaas.

Brothers (2004) is another gut-wrenching story about a Danish soldier imprisoned in Afghanistan while his wife and brother back home believe he is dead. **After the Wedding** (2006) continued her combination of local and international themes, contrasting a wealthy family in Denmark with an orphanage in India. **In a Better World** (2010) was again set between two countries, this time Denmark and Africa, and told of the barbarism that lurks underneath the surface of both. Bier was nominated for an Oscar for **After the Wedding**, and won for **In a Better World**.

Bier was less successful in bringing her trademark hyper-drama to her first US film **Things We Lost in the Fire** (2007), although she did coax strong performances from Benicio Del Toro and Halle Berry. She recently completed **All You Need Is Love** (2012), a romantic comedy written by Anders Thomas Jensen and starring Pierce Brosnan alongside Danish actresses Trine Dyrholm and Paprika Steen.

Susanne Bier

When I'm making a film, I want to be in charge. Only to a certain point, however, as there's also a part of me that doesn't want to be comfortable. I feel that it has to be a bit scary, and if you're not scared then you lose the power to get it right. It's like when you hear actors say that they have to be terrified in order to do their best work. I feel the same way as a director. I have to be terrified of the material, and on a good percentage of shooting days I need to be terrified about how I am going to get the scene to where it needs to go.

I think I had more confidence when I was very young, but by the time I realized that I shouldn't have this confidence, I had made enough films to deserve it. There are many things you need to understand as a director: obviously the technical side, and then the storytelling language, which allows you to realize when things are comprehensible, when you are overstating things, and when you can communicate without words. This starts in the writing, but the writing is only a skeleton. The meat on the bone is in the shooting, and I tend to shoot pretty slowly to make sure that I have what I need when I shoot. It is only when I edit that I like to peel it off again.

I shoot lots of different takes and also lots of different coverage, and I am more certain now of how a scene has to be drawn than I was when I first started out. I know, for example, that sometimes I wish for the opposite to what is expected. For instance, in a scene where somebody is delivering a long stretch of dialogue, traditionally you'd imagine that you'd want to watch the person who is talking, but quite often you'd be surprised how much you want to watch the listener instead. That means that you have to be just as concentrated on the person who is listening, even if there is nothing written in the script for them. Experience makes you realize that directing is much richer and less predictable than it feels.

When I started at film school, I was fortunate in that we made a lot of short films. Some were two or three minutes long, but later on they became longer and my graduation film was 43 minutes long. I was very naïve of course, but I threw myself into that film. I had a sense that if I really believed in it, it would come out right somehow, and, while it didn't all come out right—nothing ever does—I think it was a healthy energy to have because it makes you go on. It makes you survive successes and failures.

I'm very serious about what I do, but I try not to agonize about it. I don't think agonizing is necessarily creative. I do occasionally do so when I am shooting and I hardly sleep because of it. That's not enjoyable. I'm on a creative high most of the time, which is why I do what I do and I enjoy it. I liked my first film, **Freud Leaving Home**, which had clarity and a personal feel to it. I was extremely excited when making it. Exhilarated. It wasn't until it was finished that I realized that it is actually quite difficult to make a film. I threw myself into it with such abandon that I didn't quite breathe until it was over. The movie I did after that, **Family Matters (Det bli'r I familien')** (1994), was disastrous. I think that because **Freud Leaving Home** actually worked, I just walked into the next film straight away, then realized I couldn't do just that. It was a real mess. You could call it hubris on my part. You have to have a certain amount of humility with the material and on **Family Matters** I was trying to tell 80 different stories at the same time, and none of them was particularly coherent. I wasn't respectful of how clear and distinct a storyline needs to be. This has to be in the script, and I think I thought I could cover up the weaknesses in the script with the way I worked as a director. I couldn't. You can't.

By now, I have a clearer idea about what sort of script I need to have in order to make a satisfying movie. Having said that, I have just shot a romantic comedy, which was pretty frightening because I haven't shot a comedy in ages. I feel I know how to do a drama, and I think I would pretty much know how to do a thriller because I believe dramas and thrillers are closely related, but I don't have the same obvious knowledge about making a comedy. But that's why I wanted to do it—part of my artistic drive is about

> **"The meat on the bone is in the shooting, and I tend to shoot pretty slowly to make sure that I have what I need when I shoot. It is only when I edit that I like to peel it off again."**

pushing myself into some unknown land, and doing a comedy at this point in my career is certainly doing that.

The One and Only (Den eneste ene) was immensely successful; it was a blockbuster and still is. Even now you can go into a schoolyard in Denmark and hear kids quoting lines from that film. I didn't know that when I made it of course. You can't really anticipate reaction—you can test scenes and whether they communicate or not, but you can't anticipate anything like that. I always think of the audience. If you don't, you are unforgivably naïve. Film is communication; it is a mass medium. I want to tell stories that people want to hear, I don't want to craft something specifically designed for a few intellectuals in a tiny cinema.

After **The One and Only**, I realized I had to do something else altogether. I did a Swedish film called **Once in a Lifetime** (2000), but I never managed to get the script to where I thought it should be. I really loved the script initially, but it was very ambitious in terms of the stories it was trying to tell. By the time I got to **Open Hearts**, I was ready for a challenge and prepared to make a movie that wasn't necessarily going to have a big audience. I felt I needed to do something with a different kind of depth. At that point, I was considered an →

OPEN HEARTS

(01–02) Bier and Anders Thomas Jensen had done a first draft of **Open Hearts** when they were asked by Zentropa Entertainments producer Peter Aalbæk Jensen if they wanted to make it according to the minimalist Dogme manifesto (devised by Lars von Trier and Thomas Vinterberg). This would mean shooting with no sets, props, music, special effects or lighting, among other restrictions.

"I thought it would work as a Dogme film," recalls Bier, "and I don't think it would have been much different without it. I had always envisioned it as pretty rough."

Open Hearts, otherwise known as **Dogme #28**, was a valuable experience for the director. "You can only focus on the storytelling, and it's extremely educational because you realize very quickly that the call is the only important thing, and so you address that. I came away with a real enjoyment of the call of things. But then you have to do things that I found really stupid, like one character has music in her headphones and she had to really listen to it, because we couldn't layer it in afterwards. We did things just to accommodate the rules, which were not particularly creative. I enjoy the craft of layering on music. There is a real art to that or of using the costumes in the right way. That is intriguing and interesting to me."

extremely commercial director and I was making commercials as well as films. I was looking at my creative work and thinking that I had to change track, or else I would get bored and stagnant.

I felt I was doing something different with **Open Hearts**, but I think I knew that that kind of intense drama was always my strength, which is why I'm now scared of making a comedy. I think I have a certain intensity in my work that I can't help, and I think I might be like that as a person as well. Even comedy has to be based in real emotional truth. I am a great fan of crazy comedy, but I wouldn't know how to do one because at all times I would want the characters to be real. I think that's why my greatest strength is also a weakness. I am extremely intrigued by human beings; I have a lot of empathy and that comes across in my films. That's why I wouldn't want to make a film in which the lead character was an irredeemable villain, because I would try to sneak in some things that I really liked about him or her.

The way I work with [screenwriter collaborator] Anders [Thomas Jensen] is that we start out with some sort of idea or storyline. It is a very playful process. He says one thing, I say something else. We talk about one character that intrigues us and then that somehow gives ideas to other characters. It's a bit like playing with Lego. After that process he then writes—I don't

01 After the Wedding

write. Quite often we don't see each other for two or three weeks, then we sit down and talk again, and he goes off to write ten pages. I read them and I have notes, and then we discuss another 20–45 pages down the line. We don't actually make a synopsis or treatment. We make themes and we know where we think it should go, but it's never really clear until the characters are there— you can't make fully realized characters in

Collaborating

(02) Bier's longtime writing partner Anders Thomas Jensen has made his own films and written for other Danish directors such as Lone Scherfig, Søren Kragh-Jacobsen and Kristian Levring, but his best work is perhaps with Bier. "He has a very strong sense of human beings," she says. "He's very good at doing funny small things to the characters, which on paper seem a little strange, but they really work. He has a magic touch in that way."

ALL YOU NEED IS LOVE

(03–04) Bier's latest film and her first comedy in over a decade is **All You Need Is Love** starring Pierce Brosnan and Danish actress Trine Dyrholm.

"It is a comedy, but it still has some very sad things in it," she says. "The main character is a woman who has just finished treatment for breast cancer, so the story has a lot of pain. I would be happy if people laugh and cry in it at the same time."

synopsis. I don't think you can make characters in treatment either, because for me characters are very much to do with what they're saying as well.

We usually do four or five rewrites that are radically different to each other. Suddenly, between drafts one and two, a secondary character becomes the lead character. We have no inhibitions. The central idea is often only quite clear to us late in the process. We are not writing educational films, we are writing emotional films, and usually there are strong recurring themes that strike us later on in the process. I am quite possessive of the directing, although Anders comes to lunch occasionally on set. I shoot everything in the script, and then I shoot things that are not in the script.

Sometimes I change things that I feel aren't right, as in **After the Wedding**. The conversation between Rolf Lassgård's character and his wife, upon realizing that he is close to death, was written as a very comfortable scene, but two weeks into the shoot both Rolf and I felt this wasn't the right way to do it. This was a man who had been completely in control, and had succeeded in all the steps he had planned [for

his family after his death], so it didn't make sense for him to be anything other than terrified. We knew we couldn't do it the way it was written. We kept on talking about it and I kept delaying the scene, telling production to wait. Finally, Rolf and I decided that he would say a few words, and then it would be improvised. When talking about real anxiety it has to be violent, the dialogue pushed to its boundaries—so in that instance it really was about searching and figuring out what to do in a challenging, but natural way.

Since starting out I have always had a lot of respect and admiration for actors. Over the years I have learnt a common language with them, where I know what certain things mean for them, and I always love it when they do things that surprise me. At the same time, I have never been afraid of them. I've never been frightened of disagreeing with them or pushing them. Great actors always want to get there. The question is the actual arc of a scene; we want to find the less obvious or less predictable journey, which is often the most realistic or natural one.

On set, I am always struggling for a sense of truth. It has to be for real. It comes down to →

THINGS WE LOST IN THE FIRE

In Bier's last four features, the narrative has strayed out of Denmark to Afghanistan (**Brothers**), India (**After the Wedding**), Africa (**In a Better World**) and Italy (**All You Need Is Love**).

"For me it's natural to set films in different places," she explains. "I suppose part of me is stressing that our world is multicultural, and that we might as well embrace it rather than fear it. I feel, particularly in northern Europe, that we have lived in a very homogenous society."

While there are differences shooting everywhere, Bier says that the process remains the same. On **Things We Lost in the Fire** (**01–05**), she did, however, come across a different filmmaking culture. "A whole fleet of big cars would arrive at the set every day with actors and makeup," she smiles. "Superficially it was very different to what I knew, but the work was the same and I felt very comfortable with the actors. Halle Berry is a big star, but she's also a great actor and she wanted to get it right (**01, 03**). I have yet to meet the impossible actor that you see in films and I hope I never do." (**02**) Benicio Del Toro and David Duchovny also star in the film.

> "Film is communication; it is a mass medium. I want to tell stories that people want to hear, I don't want to craft something specifically designed for a few intellectuals in a tiny cinema."

costumes; set design… every single thing has to be truthful. Even if you want to heighten something—sometimes it's fun to make the costumes extreme—there's still a sense of reality. There is a fine line where you have to say "OK, now I don't believe in that character anymore." I have a pretty strong bullshit detector. One of the free gifts of being a director is that you can actually rehearse your bullshit detector in various films over the years, and you can use it in real life as well. I don't have personal experiences of a lot of the extreme situations we are dealing with. I use my own fears of those things and I have a pretty good imagination, so I guess if I wasn't making movies I would really have to see a therapist. It's not that filmmaking helps me work out issues so much, but I think I can use that fear in a creative way.

On the very intense sequences, like at the end of **Brothers**, you have to make the scene work realistically. There are certain emotions you can't keep on repeating. So once you have set up the climax and rehearsed while shooting to a certain point, you know that you have what you need and you shoot the whole take. You can't keep on pushing the button on the actors forever. It's like when you have no budget and the scene requires somebody to jump into the sea when there are only three sets of costumes. It's the same thing with emotions; you can't push that button forever.

To help get it right I always try to make things as nondramatic as possible. When I plan a sex scene, for example, I never throw out the crew. It's much better to be natural about it and still respectful. I am in awe when the actors are throwing themselves into these terrifying moments, but I try to generate a non-hysteria around them. It's more about concentrating and staying focused than it is about making a →

04 Bier with director of photography Tom Stern

05 Bier with Benicio Del Toro on the set of **Things We Lost in the Fire**

Being a woman in the film industry

The fact that there are still many more active male directors than female in the film business is, says Bier, "more a question of society than movie industry culture. I am extremely focused on efficiency in my filmmaking and I think that helps me being a director. I made a choice early on that I wanted to be both director and producer. I wanted to have my cake and eat it because I didn't want to make it seem impossible. It is a choice and a question of discipline. Having said that, I don't think my movies are defined by my gender."

> "I have a pretty strong bullshit detector. One of the free gifts of being a director is that you can actually rehearse your bullshit detector in various films over the years, and you can use it in real life as well."

drama outside the screenplay. It's pretty relaxed on set. There's no tension, but it's focused and quiet. There is no small talk—I joke with the actors all the time, but I don't have a set where people are standing in the background talking about what they had for dinner last night. That doesn't work for me.

I don't like flashy camerawork or long tracking shots. They usually end up being cut because they're slow and don't really do what I want. For me, a movie is a way of telling about life, and anything that doesn't do that isn't going to fit into the movie. I'm completely scrupulous in that regard. Even if it was the world's most complicated crane shot, if it doesn't move me emotionally it's not in the film. However, I appreciate it when I see brilliantly technical camerawork in other films, and I do think beauty is important. There have been a few landscapes in my last couple of movies, but for me they are always part of the storyline. I am interested in human beings, not technical stuff. It's why I doubt I'd ever do an action film. I watch

action films and am constantly longing for the scenes where the characters actually talk.

The first edit of each film is always pretty faithful to the structure of the script. After this I throw things around because the scripts are so solid, and have such forceful characters and conflicts that the order is less important. It's like a raw diamond that you can shape in different ways—it's not going to change even if it's cut differently.

I think I have found the rhythm now in my career. Malcolm Gladwell writes in his book *Outliers* that the point when people get really good at what they are doing is when they've spent 10,000 hours doing it. I think in my case that's probably true.

Casting unknowns

Crucial to the success of **In a Better World** was the casting of the two boys, Elias—Mikael Persbrandt and Trine Dyrholm's characters' son—and Christian, the son of Ulrich Thomsen. She cast Markus Rygaard as Elias (**02**) and William Jøhnk Juels Nielsen as Christian (**01**). Neither boy had acted before.

"I could have gotten experienced child actors, but I never do anything safely—I always do what I believe in. I knew who I had for the adults so I was looking for the boys who could be their kids, but also boys who could believably, but not predictably, be two friends. I have always felt that casting is intuitive. You feel that something is right. We did an extensive audition and when these two boys came in I was hoping they would do well in the audition. They did okay and I took a chance. They felt right and I hoped they could pull it off. I decided to help them as much as I could."

01

IN A BETTER WORLD

(01–04) The original lead character of Anton in the script of **In a Better World** was, says Bier, much more "anemic and much less masculine" than how he turned out, courtesy of charismatic actor Mikael Persbrandt **(03–04)**. "I just wanted to cast him," she says, "because he's sexy and has a brutality to him, and because that cocktail of idealism, roughness, and desirability made him a strangely vulnerable character. Casting is very important to me and I wouldn't want to make a film where I couldn't cast who I really truly believed would be right for the part." **(04)** Persbrandt with Trine Dyrholm.

Advice to young film-makers

"It may sound like a really stupid thing to say, but the best thing for filmmakers is to have a life. I think I am a bit wary of people who have been crazy about movies since the age of eight and live in the movie world. Of course there are exceptions, but in general the movies I enjoy have some relationship to life. I feel that for a director to convey life it is worthwhile to have some experience in it."

Ingmar Bergman

Perhaps the most iconic name in film history, Ingmar Bergman still represents the gold standard by which both entire careers and individual films are measured. A driven perfectionist who made over 60 films before his death in 2007, the Swedish filmmaker's raw, often devastating stories revolving around faith, betrayal, isolation and death changed filmmaking with their intense close-ups, starkly honest performances and hauntingly lit images.

His run of masterpieces is perhaps unparalleled and he is one of the few filmmakers who got better with age. His last film **Saraband**, a companion piece of sorts to **Scenes from a Marriage** made 30 years earlier, was one of his most extraordinary. Among the other greats are **Smiles of a Summer Night** (1955), **The Seventh Seal** (1957), **Wild Strawberries** (1957), **Through a Glass Darkly** (1961), **Persona** (1966), **Cries and Whispers** (1972), **Autumn Sonata** (1978), and the astonishing **Fanny and Alexander**

(1982). He worked between media, moving effortlessly from stage to film to television, and indeed both **Scenes from a Marriage** and **Fanny and Alexander** were originally TV mini-series cut down to become legendary feature films.

He worked with the same troupe of actors and many of the same department heads, notably director of photography Sven Nykvist, and lived and worked for over 40 years on the remote island of Faro in the Baltic Sea just north of Gotland.

Bergman was born in 1918, the son of a strict Lutheran pastor. He became involved in theater at Stockholm University as both an actor and a director, and became a trainee director at a theater when he graduated. He entered the film business as a script doctor at the age of 23, wrote his first screenplay for the film **Torment** in 1944 and made his directorial debut with **Crisis** in 1946.

01

01 Ingmar Bergman

> "The Swedish filmmaker's raw, often devastating stories revolving around faith, betrayal, isolation and death changed filmmaking with their intense close-ups, starkly honest performances and hauntingly lit images."

He made several films in the late 1940s, but his real breakthrough came in the 1950s with films like **Summer Interlude** (1951), **Sawdust and Tinsel** (1953), **Summer with Monika** (1953) and the exquisite comic ensemble **Smiles of a Summer Night** (1955), which was selected for competition at Cannes that year and launched him on the international stage. It was the direct influence for both Woody Allen (**A Midsummer Night's Sex Comedy**) and Stephen Sondheim (**A Little Night Music**).

By now all the films were original Bergman scripts. In 1957 both **The Seventh Seal**, a medieval story about man's relationship with God and death, and **Wild Strawberries**, a lyrical tale of an old professor looking back on his life were released. From then on, Bergman's every film became a talking point in the world's media. From his trilogy about faith—**Through a Glass Darkly**, **Winter Light** (1963) and **The Silence** (1963)—to his Oscar-winning **The Virgin Spring** (1960) and **Persona**, a bold, experimental, and visually daring piece that questioned the fragmented nature of identity.

By now he had a group of actors that he employed in all his films, including Max von Sydow, Gunnar Björnstrand, Harriet Andersson, Bibi Andersson, Liv Ullmann, Gunnel Lindblom, and Erland Josephson.

Other films from this period include **Shame** (1968), **The Passion of Anna** (1969), **Cries and Whispers** (1972), and his blockbusting TV series **Scenes from a Marriage** (1973), which was Sweden's TV event of the decade. He left Sweden, however, after a charge of tax evasion in 1976 and made films in Germany and Norway (including a film in English; **The Serpent's Egg**; and the classic **Autumn Sonata** starring Ingrid Bergman and Liv Ullmann) before returning in 1978.

In 1982, he made perhaps his most beloved work, **Fanny and Alexander**, a 312-minute TV series, cut down for theatrical release to a 188-minute film, in which Bergman revisits his childhood in a supremely satisfying saga of joy and pain, which was intended as his final major work. He worked continuously after that in theater and on TV, and some of those TV films, like **After the Rehearsal** (1984) and **Saraband** (2003), are as rigorous and vital as anything he had made before. He died at the age of 89 on Faro in 2007.

02 Bibi Andersson and Liv Ullmann in **Persona**

03 Liv Ullmann and Ingrid Bergman in **Autumn Sonata**

04 Gunnar Björnstrand and Ingrid Thulin in **Wild Strawberries**

Nuri Bilge Ceylan

"I am a control freak, I suppose. You have to be,
because the director is the only person on the set
who understands and knows the complete film."

A brilliant filmmaker from Turkey who has exploded onto the global scene in the last decade, Nuri Bilge Ceylan made his short and first few features in a do-it-yourself fashion with minuscule budgets, but their visual beauty and profoundly personal subject matter earned them immediate attention.

His third feature **Uzak** (**Distant**), made in 2002, focused on themes of country and city values in its story of a young factory worker who travels to Istanbul from the countryside to stay with a relative who is an intellectual photographer. It was selected for competition at the Cannes Film Festival in 2003 and was considered a masterpiece, winning Ceylan the Grand Jury Prize and his two lead actors sharing the Best Actor prize.

In his 2006 drama **Climates**, he played the lead role, and his real-life wife Ebru Ceylan played his character's estranged girlfriend. Beloved by some critics more than **Uzak**, it again played in Cannes competition and won the FIPRESCI critics prize for best film. Its portrait of the subtle cruelties and self-absorption of relationships is quietly devastating.

His fifth film, **Three Monkeys** (2008), was a departure of sorts, telling a more melodramatic story of a family torn apart when the father is bribed into taking responsibility for a murder he didn't commit. Atmospheric and ravishingly beautiful, it won him the best director award at Cannes.

Once Upon a Time in Anatolia (2011) is his sixth film, his fourth consecutive film to play in competition in Cannes, and his most ambitious to date. A near three-hour story about a murder investigation set over one night and the following morning, it again explores profound issues of the damage wrought by relationships and desire. It too won him the Grand Jury Prize at Cannes, lodging him firmly in the very highest echelons of visionary filmmakers.

Nuri Bilge Ceylan

" I started out in photography because in those days in Turkey, cinema was the domain of a few specific people and it was so expensive because there was no digital technology or video cameras to bring the cost down. I started taking photographs quite early on, when I was about 15 years old in Istanbul. In those days there was no art around me at all, but when I was 15 someone gave me a book about photography and darkroom techniques as a present, and it looked less like art than a game to me. I started some printing in the bathroom and it was like magic seeing the photograph coming out in the red light.

After my military service, I went to England to study, but I didn't have enough money so instead I watched lots of films at the Scala Cinema in King's Cross and the NFT on the South Bank. The Scala used to show two or three movies a day with one ticket and I would go and see these films almost every day. Watching movies was the best education for me. If you understand the technical side a little bit, as I did, you can watch a movie and figure out which lens they used, the position of the camera, what they were doing in each scene. What the director did was more mystical for me, because I didn't know exactly what went on behind a camera and I had never been on a set before.

When I came back to Turkey in my late 20s, I went to film school for two years, but left as I felt it was not really necessary. Because there were no video cameras around yet, we couldn't practice. My taste and understanding of movies was quite different from that of the teachers and the other students generally. So I felt rather alone in university and in the world, but during that period, one of my friends, who was not from the university, made a short film and asked me to act in it. So I acted in it and in return I joined him in post-production, which taught me a lot, and then I bought the very old camera that had been used in that short film—an Arriflex 2B, which can shoot movies without sound—for $3,000.

Some time later I began to shoot my short film, just like I used to practice photography, shooting my family working in the fields or animals around. I shot everything on 35mm, which was expensive, and with time I also realized that I needed a focus puller, so I asked a friend to do it and he used very primitive methods. I just shot my short film like that and sent it to Cannes, and they selected it in the short film competition among ten movies.

Later, with the same methods, I shot my first feature **Kasaba** (**The Small Town**) with only one assistant, again as a focus puller, and my family and friends as the actors. I used to have what most of the filmmakers don't have, which is time. I spent at least a year making this film. I went to my childhood town to go on shooting whenever I was free. In those days I used to make a living taking pictures for ceramic catalogs, like the character in **Uzak**.

So it all started because I felt that I could practice cinema without needing many people around me.

For editing, I bought a Prévost editing machine, which was so big that it basically filled a whole room in my house. We managed it somehow, even though this was before digital post-production came in. But I wasn't happy with the post stage, so on the second film, I began to understand what materials and coverage I needed. I learned from my mistakes. I had to shoot with real sound because with real sound you can improvise within certain limits, which is very important when you are working with amateurs. Professional actors know how to get the gist of the script, but with amateurs you have to be free. My scripts are not like the bible, and I found the amateur actors in **Kasaba** so much richer on set than the words I wrote in the script. Out of the blue they would say or do something so original during shooting that that evening I would change other parts of the script.

For my second film, **Clouds of May** (1999), I bought another camera that lets you shoot sync with sound. I needed a camera with a timecode that can be synced with the dat recorder. I didn't like to use a clapperboard because sometimes I needed to shoot secretly and with a clap →

> "Sound is very important. One scene can tell a completely different story with a different sound design. You can completely change the meaning of the scene by changing the sound."

CLIMATES

(01–05) Ceylan laughs that Turkish critics didn't rate his performance as Isa in **Climates**, although he says "I don't think it was that bad because I know this kind of character very well." He cast his wife Ebru in the role of Bahar (**01, 03, 05**). "I had to cast her because, since I was not working behind the camera, I felt I should act with somebody I really trusted, who knows me and what I say." For Ceylan, Isa's behavior toward Bahar is understandable, although many who watch it consider him reprehensible. "Most of the critics of **Climates** say that he is a bastard, but I think all of us are like that and we find it hard to accept. It's easy to deceive ourselves and not confess. I wanted to show that it is like that for most of us."

When Isa leaves Bahar, says Ceylan, "he couldn't find the balance that he missed inside himself. He thought that when he left her, life would be much better because she was the problem in his life, but when he couldn't find the meaning in life after that, it created a violence in him. He goes back to her because he's still not sure if he wants her or not, then leaves her again because he doesn't know what he wants. The most difficult thing for a man at this age is to understand what he wants and that is the problem of excess freedom. He has money, freedom, and respect and if you are free to choose anything, it's difficult to make a choice. That is often why village people are happier and don't have such problems, because they have responsibilities and are not free to choose that much."

The power of **Climates** lies in the small details of the relationship and the small hurts that are committed in an effort to find individual happiness. "I find these kinds of things the biggest problems in my life," says Ceylan, "and I have felt the pain of choosing a lifestyle for myself and trying to understand what I want."

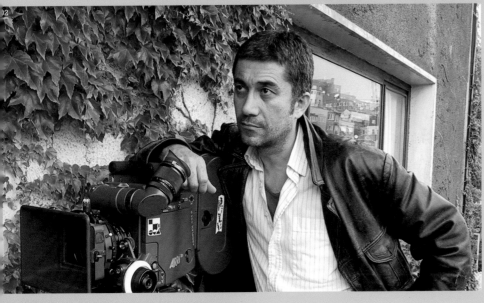

UZAK

(01–07) This film was originally a much longer script and Ceylan shot many sequences he never used, including a whole subplot about a murder that takes place in the apartment upstairs. "I left the murder out because I didn't want it to be the dominant factor," he explains. "Similarly, I shot lots of different endings, such as Yusuf going to work in a mine, because that was the only job he could find. I decided that the one I used was more simple and I didn't want to change the essence of the film."

The photographer character in the film, Mahmut, may be a city sophisticate, but says Ceylan, he has disconnected from his art. "He has a business and earns money, but has lost connection with what he wants to do, which is make movies. To make movies you need lots of energy, you need to sacrifice your easy life and your comfort zone, which he can't do. That's why small-town people amaze me sometimes. They can very easily sacrifice themselves. They can be very cruel sometimes and can kill easily. They have all the elements that make people human. With educated people they are never that cruel, but they don't sacrifice anything either. They don't do anything. Mahmut's mother lives very close to him in **Uzak**, but he doesn't have much in common with her, while Yusuf is passionate about his family."

Using the elements to your advantage

(05–07) The scenes of snowy Istanbul in **Uzak** are among the most beautiful in cinema and Ceylan only shot them when, by chance, it snowed. "You never know whether it will snow in Istanbul or not. I didn't use them to make it beautiful, but I like atmospheric situations. It makes you feel that there is a cosmic dimension to life. You feel what kind of world you live in, so I like to underline the situation with atmosphere like rain, snow and wind."

everyone knows that you are shooting. So I bought an Aaton 35 camera from the factory in France. On the second film, we had five people in the crew—me, a focus puller, a sound person, one production person, and one joker. I operated the camera, and again I used my family and friends as the actors.

The money that I spent was only about $100,000. I raised the budget myself: I didn't want to ask for support from anyone because nobody knew who I was at the time and I knew that the film I wanted to make was not exactly what the market needed. Fortunately, I was able to sell my second feature to TV for a small amount of money, as well as making some foreign sales, and I got the money back. With that film, I really began to know what cinema meant to me and how I wanted to shoot my films.

I suppose there is a variation of my own character in each of the films because I want to express myself in them. These characters are quite self-critical. I feel jealous in general when I meet small-town people because they are really balanced in themselves and I try to understand why. What did I lose by being an intellectual or this kind of personality? My films are a kind of therapy, in a way.

Anyway, by the time I made **Uzak**, I was much more confident and well prepared. I shot it in my own house in Istanbul where I was living alone after my marriage of seven years broke down. Before I shot it, when I was writing the script, I used to shoot photographs of every possible angle, stick these small photographs on the pages of the script and use them to think of a →

mise-en-scène. I was really very confident about this film when I started shooting. I knew the actors well and the actors knew me because I had worked with them before.

It was probably my easiest movie technically. One day, by chance, it started snowing and I was able to modify the script to include the snow. We shot the snow scenes in three days. We had five people and two actors. For the snow scenes, we only needed one actor, so there were six of us and not much equipment. One car was enough to move around fast, and we managed to shoot everything in three days. It cost about $100,000 again to make **Uzak**, but of course I did not take any fee as usual, and the camera and the sound equipment was mine. Fortunately, non-linear editing suites were more common by then and we could edit the film at home like when we did **Clouds of May**.

It was more difficult with the next film **Climates**, mainly because I decided to act in it myself, so we had to increase the crew. I also decided to shoot it with a digital camera for the first time. I rented a camera from a company that could also provide an operator. His name was Gökhan Tiryaki and that was his first feature film. Since then we have worked together in all my films. We had to have him because I was acting in nearly every frame of the movie. It was a very difficult shooting period because we shot on many locations around Turkey and we were dependent on the weather. The crew was made up of twelve people this time. For the winter and snow scenes we went to the coldest region of Turkey in February, but it didn't snow. We waited for three weeks and in the end we had to go to other places to search for the snow because the script called for it. It meant that we had to mix up footage of different towns: the characters were walking in a street from one city and in the next shot they were walking in another city, but it was all meant to be the same city. It was the magic of cinema. There was more artifice in the process. The editing was also a mess. I shot a lot of footage because of the freedom of the digital camera. Tapes were, of course, much cheaper than film.

Sound is very important. One scene can tell a completely different story with a different sound design. You can completely change the meaning of the scene by changing the sound. I don't like to express the meaning of the films just by the expressions of the characters. But with sound, you can modify whether the character is happy or melancholic in a certain scene.

I like the sound of nature. It is like music for me. Perhaps because of that I don't feel like using music as such because it hides the natural sounds. I basically make a rough sound design during off-line editing—because the sound will affect the length of the shots you want to edit.

In **Uzak**, I remember in the editing, I searched around for the sound of the mouse in the apartment. The sound of a real mouse squeaking was not good enough, so I searched for different kinds of bird sounds for the mouse and processed them in many different ways. I always make the sound design myself, but since **Climates** I also work with a sound editor. He puts in what he sees as important himself and I put in what I see as important, and then we mix them.

Having said that, facial expressions are getting more important to me. In real life, facial expressions can tell you everything if you are the kind of person who can understand them. Some details of a facial expression can help you understand the truth and you shouldn't rely on or believe in what people say because everybody protects themselves with words. They try to make themselves more important or heroic. I think in films we should not just believe what the characters say. The characters should often say innocent lies as in life. The reality or the truth should lie rather in the facial expressions and other details, so recently I tend to do more close-ups and focus on facial expressions and the position of the body. In my early days, I shot wider, but now I shoot more closely and acting is of more importance.

It's often best to shoot different levels of expression and later in the editing decide on the right one. First I shoot what I wrote in the →

THREE MONKEYS

(01–05) After **Uzak** and **Climates**, Ceylan employed fewer autobiographical elements and mainly professional actors in **Three Monkeys**. "I have some problems with professionals because a lot of the time they have habits that are hard to break, but sometimes I like them because they are very disciplined," he says. "They really like to act and they have a real passion for acting, whereas amateurs get bored more easily. I still like to use a mixture of professional and amateur actors, but it depends on the project."

Three Monkeys, he says, was "a much more controlled movie. I was more confident making it because, after **Climates**, I was back behind the camera. My greatest confidence comes in the editing because, like in **Climates**, I had shot a lot of footage on digital and I spend a lot of time over the editing."

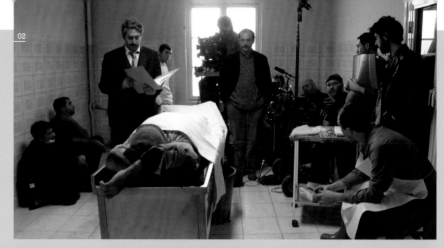

ONCE UPON A TIME IN ANATOLIA

(**01–05**) This film marked a departure of sorts for Ceylan, since it features myriad characters and required a crew of over 70 people. But it wasn't just the escalating cost that made it a risky proposition: much of the film is set in the Anatolian countryside in near pitch darkness (**01**). Although Ceylan found the experience nerve-wracking, the film was declared a masterpiece when it was unveiled in competition at Cannes 2011. (**03**) Ceylan with Gökhan Tiryaki, the director of photography he has collaborated with since **Climates**.

script, then I begin to shoot different levels of expression and sometimes shoot the opposite of what I intended. Editing is really the only place where you can judge which one works. In the editing, I can understand if a shot works or not in one second. In the shooting, it is harder to judge it. I never watch dailies. Instead of watching dailies, I prefer to shoot one more take.

Once Upon a Time in Anatolia is quite different for me. It has a lot of characters in it and it was more expensive to make than all the other films put together. We just wrote the script and didn't realize that it would cost that much because I am not very good at calculating things like that. We got some support from Eurimages and started shooting, but we had to spend a lot of our own money. It was quite risky.

Even though I have won awards at festivals, a Turkish movie is still a hard sell in distribution terms. But I feel like I can manage. I don't complain at all. I know that I make difficult movies and my new movie is even more difficult than before. It's two and a half hours long. Plus half of the film is set at night and it mostly centers on men—there are not many women in it. These are things that don't appeal to buyers.

It was a different experience for me to be behind the camera with a crew of 70 and shooting in the middle of nowhere in complete darkness. There were a lot of actors; we were shooting in the middle of the night and it was extremely cold, so the actors needed caravans to warm up in. We needed portable toilets and a lot of lights because there was no light. The

The benefits of digital video

Nuri Bilge Ceylan and Bora Gökşingöl during an editing session of **Once Upon a Time in Anatolia** in Ceylan's office (**05**).

"I don't think I will go back to film again. I feel that you can search for new ways of expression and you can have a chance to go deeper into the human soul with digital just because you can shoot more in low-budget independent movies. You can try many different things in the shooting and in editing, something you never intended to be a magical moment becomes one. It's good to have that much material in editing if you are after something indefinable and something ambiguous."

only light sources were supposed to be the headlights of the cars.

I didn't like the feeling of having so many crew members. More mistakes are made because they don't really know what I want. The communication chains are easily broken. This can often lead to misunderstandings. You say something to your assistant and he says something to his assistant, and he talks to the sound engineer, but your message entirely changes.

I am a control freak, I suppose. You have to be, because the director is the only person on the set who understands and knows the complete film. The technical crew concentrates only on the shot they are doing at that moment, but you know how to relate it to other parts of the film. I try to keep myself free of other people's expectations all the

time. In my head, I try to return to the feelings of the good old days when I first started making movies. Of course, this is perhaps not possible, but I try.

I don't give exaggerated meanings to awards at film festivals. As an artist, you are living in the underground, by yourself and all alone. When you are shooting, in reality, you are all alone because nobody really understands what you are intending, not even the person closest to you.

Jean-Pierre Dardenne and Luc Dardenne

"Of course there is a fine line between reality and the fact that cinema is illusion. The characters we are focusing on don't exist... We find our inspiration in real life, but they are all fictional."

Brothers Jean-Pierre and Luc Dardenne were born in the French-speaking region of Liège in Belgium, Jean-Pierre in 1951 and Luc in 1954. They have worked together as a writing-producing-directing team since the 1970s and have become known in the last fifteen years for the unadorned naturalism and social realism of their potent dramas, often telling of people—unemployed, immigrants, criminals, homeless—on the margins of Belgian society.

They founded the production company Derives in 1975 and through it made over sixty documentary features and shorts, which dealt with many of the social issues that would reappear in their fictional work later on. They experimented with narrative in the little-seen **Falsch** (1987) and **Je pense à vous** (1992), but it was **The Promise [La Promesse]** (1996) that cemented their reputation as great storytellers. The story of a young boy—played by then newcomer Jérémie Renier—and his involvement with some African immigrants exploited by his unscrupulous father—played by Olivier Gourmet—the film was the first of an unbroken run of riveting dramas examining the less privileged and those exploiting them.

The subsequent films, all set in their hometown of Seraing are **Rosetta** (1999), **The Son** (2002), **The Child** (2005), **The Silence of Lorna** (2008), and **The Kid with a Bike** (2011). They were all selected for official competition in Cannes, and both **Rosetta** and **The Child** won the Palme d'Or, casting the Dardennes into a club of only six filmmakers to win the coveted award twice.

Renier and Gourmet have become staple actors in the Dardenne brothers' films, and Gourmet appears in cameos (**The Child**, **The Kid with a Bike**) when there is no role for him. Similarly, the brothers work consistently with the same collaborators, such as cinematographer Alain Marcoen, production designer Igor Gabriel, and editor Marie-Hélène Dozo.

Jean-Pierre Dardenne and Luc Dardenne

LUC The Kid with a Bike is a good example of how we go about making a film.

The starting point was a story we heard of that took place in the suburbs of Tokyo. We had gone to Tokyo to present **The Son** in 2003 and at a screening we met a judge who specializes in childhood issues and told us the whole story. It was about a boy, around ten years old, who had been abandoned by his father. The boy was left in an orphanage and the father promised that he would come for him later, but obviously he never showed up. The boy escaped from the orphanage several times and the judge we met was in charge of the boy, who by then was a teenager and had trouble integrating into society.

Jean-Pierre and I kept talking and bringing up that story for several years, but without finding a thread to turn it into a screenplay. Then, after we had made **The Child** and **The Silence of Lorna**, we embarked on another story about a female doctor who took care of children. That was when we thought we could mix up the two stories. We chose to make the woman, who was originally a doctor, a hairdresser, because it was a little bit contrived and obvious if she was a doctor and then had her taking charge of the child.

That's how we started out. We thought it would be interesting to deal with this tense encounter between this young child and this woman who was a hairdresser, so in the end, it's a combination of a real-life story and a fiction that we invented.

JEAN-PIERRE When we are writing our scripts, we talk a lot. On **The Kid with a Bike**, we spent a few months just talking between the two of us. We had the three main characters that we had decided to focus on, so we just kept chatting and chatting. And yet, at the time, we didn't actually know how the story would end. There were a couple of options and we still hadn't settled on the one we wanted. Either—and this is what you see in the final edit of the film—the boy falls from the tree and gets up and cycles home, or you have him fall from the tree and die.

We thought that Samantha's love was strong enough that Cyril should be able to get up, leave his father and the lying son behind in the woods and get back to Samantha's house. An end to the film in the manner of Chaplin. Until then, we thought that Cyril would die because we didn't know what to do with the man and his son. If Cyril woke up, we didn't want a reconciliation scene between the three of them, which would have been too easy and angelic. At that moment, we didn't think that Cyril was able to pass in front of them and leave them with their lie.

LUC When we started talking about the story, we immediately envisioned the locations where we could shoot. There are three main locations—the council housing, the woods, and the gas station—and these are locations that we know that actually exist. We knew that our characters would go from one place to the other. The gas station was turned into a grocery store for the sake of our story. We talked and talked for eight months and were still wavering between focusing on the young boy or maybe starting the film out with another story, and we kept on going back and forth. That was how the first structure for the storyline came about. It was a very gradual process. When we had this first draft of the structure, my brother [Jean-Pierre] started writing the actual screenplay.

JEAN-PIERRE I write the dialogue and finalize the first draft, which I would then send to Luc and he would make his remarks and corrections, and then send it back to me and I'd send it back to him, and so on and so forth. By the time we are at the seventh or eighth version of the script we send it to the executive producer and the French producing partner. Depending on what they say, we take their remarks into consideration and sometimes include them, sometimes not. Sometimes, of course, they are right and sometimes we think we're right. Then we edit a new version of the script.

We don't like improvisation with actors on set much. Once the dialogue is written, it's not open to change. We have one or two months of

> "We also use a lot of long shots, sequence shots where we hide things in the shot that are concealed to start with, but which are gradually revealed to the audience. It's something used by other filmmakers as well, but we like it a lot."

rehearsals before the shooting and things come up then. We realize that we've made some mistakes here and there, and so we make these changes in the screenplay and that is the version we use to shoot.

LUC We shoot in continuity. We start the shoot with scene one and, even though the screenplay may change during shooting and what happens during the shoot may influence the final film, we know that things will make sense as we go along and it will all fall into place. Even though we are shooting in continuity, we keep the locations intact so that, if something changes in the storyline during the shoot, we can go back to the previous scene and the previous location and do a retake. In the case of **The Kid with a Bike**, nothing changed and we remained pretty close to the original screenplay.

Other times, the whole story structure can be affected during shooting. In the original screenplay of **Rosetta**, the mother character was far more important than in the final film. Largely over the course of the shooting, the significance of the mother dwindled and in the end it's virtually non-existent.

Likewise, the ending of **The Son** changed completely. As it was written, the brawl was supposed to happen in the woods when Gourmet attempted to strangle Morgan Marinne, playing the man who had killed his son, but didn't go through with it. In the original script, Gourmet was going to get up and faint, and then Marinne would go to the car, open the trunk and get the flask of coffee that we had previously seen in the film and give him a drink of coffee. So originally we were going to go back to that flask of coffee, and the film would end like that.

But we realized that if we ended the film like that, it wouldn't be right. We were trying to do that scene just to bring the coffee back into the drama. However, the characters had left a car that was meant to be loaded up with boards of wood, so this car had to serve some kind of purpose. We ended up having the two characters lifting boards of wood onto the car. That way we are

ending it in a more efficient, less literal way. The characters would be reunited in a working context. So we were happy that we ended up with something less literary and more character-driven. If we used the coffee, it would be pointing to a previous scene in the movie where it had been used. That would be us trying to be auteur-like.

JEAN-PIERRE We do everything we can to steer ourselves away from that auteurish self-consciousness in the writing, the dialogue, the directing of the actors, the mise-en-scène. Whatever it takes, we don't want any staging effects. We try to capture what is most difficult and not be emphatic or pompous about it but very simple—which can be difficult. Of course, the camerawork is a writing tool and we are making a statement with the camerawork, but the camerawork is not done in a random fashion. If, for example, there is a lot of tension between two characters and the camera goes from one to the other, what we are trying to do is embrace and create that tension. One example is in **Rosetta**, →

01 Jérémie Renier as Bruno in **The Child**

"We do everything we can to steer ourselves away from that auteurish self-consciousness in the writing, the dialogue, the directing of the actors, the mise-en-scène. Whatever it takes, we don't want any staging effects."

when there is a brawl at the beginning. We are not trying to do multiple camera movements just for the hell of it or just to have the audience feel like there is a lot of movement and action. Or in **The Promise**, when the girl takes the radio back and they know the father is dead, there is a very slow camera movement. We are trying to announce the tension literally with that camera motion.

Of course, there is a fine line between reality and the fact that cinema is illusion. The characters we are focusing on don't exist and we have invented them, even though we are trying to insert them in reality. We find our inspiration in real life, but they are all fictional. And as Luc says, life goes on around the characters and we try to capture that life as it happens, so, especially in the rehearsal process, the storyline can change.

We also use a lot of long shots, sequence shots where we hide things in the shot that are concealed to start with, but which are gradually revealed to the audience. It's something used by other filmmakers as well, but we like it a lot. What we are trying to do is have the viewer expect something, make the viewer want to know what's

going to happen. He doesn't know who's behind the door, for example, but he definitely wants to find out. Then maybe later on in the film, we will tell him who is behind the door.

When the film starts, something has happened already and there will be a delay before we find out what it is. This is what captures the viewer's attention and that's what makes the viewer want to know more about the characters. When we shot Assita's arrival in **The Promise** in the lobby, we didn't frame her to show that she was going to play a significant part in the film. What we frame is the lobby itself and the immigrants in it, then Olivier and Jérémie, and then, as it happens, Assita finds herself in the frame. What we are trying to say is that even if we had not been there to shoot her, she would have been there all the same. She just happens to be there—the other characters don't make it happen. It's mise-en-scène in disguise and comes from our background in documentaries.

LUC In a way, it's about the illusion of reality. We want to give the viewer the illusion that things would have happened had the camera been

01–02 The Son

The rehearsal process

The brothers' rehearsal process with actors can last from four weeks to eight weeks. "During our first rehearsals with the actors, we try to help them abandon everything that makes them comfortable and keeps them in the image they have of themselves," they explain. "A professional actor will be tempted to protect his or her image as an actor, a non-professional will be tempted unconsciously to protect the image he has of himself in his life. It is necessary that they abandon these images that close them in—that they let them go. Our job is to enable this abandonment, mainly by creating an environment where we are all equals and they have no fear of appearing foolish or of suggesting ideas that might appear uninteresting. As long as the director shows that he is trying, searching and not pretending to know the truth, the actors should put their trust in him and suggest things that they wouldn't have dared to suggest, that would never even have occurred to them otherwise."

The Dardennes continue: "In the first rehearsals, we work especially on the body—on walking, stopping, turning around, walking up and down stairs, opening and closing doors, falling over, getting up from a sleeping position to a standing position, handling props and clothes, physical contact for fights or embracing. The result is that we see the actors engaged in the everyday, automatic actions of life and not in performance. We don't treat the professional and non-professional actors any differently. The non-professional learns from the professional's experience and the professional learns from the presence of the non-professional, which does not depend on technique. When we work with an actor who has never acted before and who has a principal role—like Émilie Dequenne in Rosetta or Thomas Doret (03) in **The Kid with a Bike**—we make time to work with

03 Jean-Pierre and Luc directing Cyril, played by Thomas Doret, in **The Kid with a Bike**

them alone to rehearse gestures and find the rhythm of actions while they are speaking and while they are silent. It is a period in which we are looking at them, taming them, giving them trust. During these long rehearsals, which last a month or two, the moments when we are not working or when we are resting, when we are walking to a location or in the car are as important to establish friendship and trust. Also important are the moments with the costume designer when we try on their clothes. The sessions last one or two hours and there are at least three a week. It is during these fittings that the character constructs itself for them as much for us, to get ready to enter the film."

there or not to record these characters. Of course, it's all an illusion, but we are trying to film events as if they are not contrived, so it looks like we haven't positioned this actor on the left of the frame and the other one on the right so they can start a conversation. It just comes up on the frame and they happen to be there, and if the camera had not been around, they would still exist.

Of course, this is not easy to achieve and all depends on the actors we work with. For instance, some of our actors are newcomers and have never been in front of a camera before. When we first worked with Jérémie Renier, he

had never been on film before. On the other hand, we worked with Cécile De France (on **The Kid with a Bike**) and she is a very established actress. The actors and the characters are doing something most of the time, the scenes are action-oriented. It's very rare that you see two actors engaging in a long conversation, for example. Even when they do have a long conversation, they have something else to do at the same time. That comes from the rehearsal process where we have the actors do this specifically. This focus on action is what we are always trying to achieve. →

Using what is familiar to you

Each of the Dardenne brothers' films takes place in their hometown of Seraing and the surrounding area. "We think of our scenarios in relation to the town, we imagine the places where the action takes place or where the characters live. If Belgium plays a role, it would be more in terms of language because we do not speak French like they do in France, so it is important that an actor or actress who is often working in Paris lose their Parisian accent to appear in our films so as not to appear foreign in Seraing. If this town nourishes our cinema, it is probably because the memories of our childhood and adolescence circulate together in it."

01–02 Émilie Dequenne
as Rosetta in **Rosetta**

JEAN-PIERRE Fundamentally we are trying to keep away from what we see in most movies where the actors all behave in a certain way. In most movies, it's attitude-oriented and that's something we are trying to keep away from. We are aiming for actors to be action-oriented: they are doing something, they are not posing, not putting on an attitude or pretending that they are doing something. We are not into pretence. They are actually doing it. In rehearsal, we work with the actors as if there is no camera. We pretend that there is no urgent viewpoint, so if they have to hide something, they will hide it and if that means you don't see their face anymore, that's fine. Professional actors will usually enquire about the position of the camera and we just tell them to ignore the camera. There is no camera. If you have to fight with someone, just fight with them, don't think about where the camera is. It's a very liberating process because the actors abandon themselves during the rehearsal process and that's how we find the location of the camera for when we shoot later on. But we are trying to avoid the "right place" for the camera so that the actor appears in their best light.

LUC In **The Kid with a Bike**, there is a scene in a car where the boy is scratching his face and he throws himself into the woman's arms. When we were shooting it, his arm was always in the way, blocking the view, so we had to lift the camera a little to capture the boy cuddling in her arms. So what started out as an obstacle became a new mise-en-scène, a new way of filming the boy. We discovered it during the rehearsal process.

JEAN-PIERRE Spontaneity for an actor is wishful thinking. Whatever attitude or gesture I want the actor to make, it has to become totally automatic for the actor. It has to be organically conceived and the only way for that is to have a significant number of rehearsals. That way, the actor can just be. We will not be acting precisely. That's what we are aiming for: not acting.

LUC We do everything together. We complement each other and, depending on whether we have a monitor or not, our two visions can complement each other. For instance, if one of us is standing by the camera and one of us is standing by the monitor, we can become complementary. It's very important for us to create a kind of shrine on the set just for the two of us where we can talk between ourselves about what we have just shot. We confer together and nobody else is consulted besides the two of us. That togetherness, which is so important, is then reactivated after shooting the scene where we were a little bit separated. Apart from that moment when we shoot a scene, we are separated at no other time.

03 Jean-Pierre and Luc filming **The Silence of Lorna** (also shown here are Jérémie Renier, Natali Tabareau, Arta Dobroshi and Marika Piedboeuf)

04–05 Arta Dobroshi and Jérémie Renier in **The Silence of Lorna**

Guillermo del Toro

"Being from Mexico is an enormous part of who I am as a filmmaker. The panache, the sense of melodrama, and the madness I have in my movies that allows me to mix historical events with fictional creatures, all comes from an almost surreal Mexican sensibility."

One of the leaders of the Mexican new wave that exploded onto the global scene in the 1990s and one of the most imaginative filmmakers at work anywhere in the world today, Guillermo del Toro travels between languages and budget ranges, between the independent sector and Hollywood. Born in 1964, Del Toro started his film career in his teens studying makeup design under Hollywood master Dick Smith (**The Exorcist**) and executive produced his first feature, the now classic gay comedy **Doña Herlinda and Her Son** (1985), at the tender age of 21. He was a makeup supervisor for most of his twenties with his own company Necropia, but also made ten shorts and directed 13 TV episodes.

His first feature **Cronos** (1993) illustrated his passion for dark fantasy and horror, and was a huge international success, winning the FIPRESCI prize at Cannes. It won him his first filmmaking deal in Hollywood directing the giant bug movie **Mimic** (1997), although the experience left him bruised and he returned to Mexico to make **The Devil's Backbone** (2001), an unsettling ghost story set against the Spanish Civil War. His second experience in Hollywood was more positive, taking on **Blade II** (2002) and the supernatural comic book adventure **Hellboy** (2004), before returning to the Spanish Civil War setting for his superb **Pan's Labyrinth** (2006). Selected for competition at Cannes and winner of three Oscars, the film is a magical, violent, and moving blend of harsh reality and fantasy that sealed his name as a creative master. He flipped back to Hollywood subsequently for **Hellboy II: The Golden Army** (2008), before accepting the task of directing two films based on J.R.R. Tolkien's **The Hobbit** for producer Peter Jackson. However, delays meant Del Toro had to move onto other projects. Jackson has since taken over the directing reins. Del Toro nevertheless has co-writing credits on both.

Del Toro has a production partnership with his Mexican pals Alfonso Cuarón and Alejandro González Iñárritu, and has nurtured and produced many new talented directors. He is currently in production on the epic science-fiction movie **Pacific Rim** (2013), in which enormous robots are deployed by humans to battle an attack by massive aliens.

Guillermo del Toro

I came from the provinces, from Guadalajara, which is the second largest city in Mexico and nobody makes movies there. When I was a teenager, I started building relationships in Mexico City and I started as a blue-collar member of the crew. I was either a boom guy or a PA or an assistant director. I was makeup effects. I did my floor time in both TV and movies. My first professional work on a movie was at the age of 16 and I made **Cronos** when I was 28, so I had twelve solid years of doing just about everything in between. If somebody needed something, I would do it. I even did illegal stunt driving. But what happened is that I learned a little bit of everything and, once you put your time into exploring everything, you get to know what every piece of grip equipment is called and how many you need, and how to do post—I edited my own movies and did the post sound effects on all of them. So to some extent, directing came naturally to me from my first movie.

My first movie **Cronos** is not in any way a perfect movie, but it's a movie full of conviction. When you make your first movie, whatever mistakes you make are very glaring, but if you have conviction, and I would even say cinematic faith, this also shines through. I recently watched **Cronos** again and I thought, "I like this kid," he has possibilities. After your first movie, with a little bit of craft, diligence, and more importantly, experience, you learn to make virtues out of some of your defects.

What I mean is that any first movie has good moments, even if it is not entirely perfect. It can be a filmmaker as famous as you like, such as Stanley Kubrick, whose first film **Fear and Desire** (1953) is about 70 minutes long and stars Paul Mazursky. It is very stilted, very awkwardly paced, full of stuff that doesn't work, the actors speak in a patois, and it has a very non-naturalistic rhythm. But what is incredibly fascinating is that the very stilted quality, that artificial rhythm, eventually became his trademark in later films. He bypasses it in more naturalistic films like **The Killing** (1956) and **Paths of Glory** (1957), but comes back to that type of hyperrealism or strange filtered reality in his later movies, and he is in complete control of it there. Kubrick used the tools he acquired in making other films to transform what you thought was a defect in **Fear and Desire** into a virtue.

In my case, when I make movies in Spanish, starting with **Cronos**, I purposefully avoid characterizing certain things in the conventional Hollywood sense, and that comes out as a blatant defect. Specifically, I had shot a much longer film, including a whole section between the husband and wife where she noticed that he is getting younger and they start falling in love again. At night, he would come and sleep underneath her bed. But I couldn't make it work. The way I staged it was simply too stilted and strange, and I didn't feel comfortable leaving it as part of the movie. Even to this day, I think there is a mix of different tones in that movie. I change from the dramatic to the comedic too often. I try to do it generically, mixing horror with melodrama, and there are moments in **Cronos** that are really jarring for me. I sometimes allowed Ron Perlman to be too broad and it simply didn't work. I think I did it better in my later movies.

I don't know whether that mix of genres is my trademark. One of the things that was very influential for me when I was kid was the book by Tolkein in which he discussed fairy stories in literature. I remember him saying in that book that you should make the story recognizable enough to be rooted in reality, but outlandish enough to be a flight of fancy. So I try to mix an almost prosaic approach, or at least a rigid historical context, with fantastic elements. I treat the fantasy characters very naturalistically or else I root the story in a precise context like **The Devil's Backbone** or **Pan's Labyrinth**, or in **Cronos**, post-NAFTA Mexico.

As Tolkien says, when you give the audience a taste of what they can recognize, they immediately accept the rest of the concoction; it's almost like wrapping a pill in bacon for a dog to swallow it. You need, for example, the bacon of domesticity in **Cronos**. I wanted to shoot that family as a very middle-class family in Mexico.

> "Directing is almost like keeping four balls in the air on a monocycle with a train approaching behind you."

I wanted a kitchen that looked like a kitchen you'd recognize, a really ordinary bedroom and very mild, neat clothing design. Out of that middle-class reality, I wanted a single anomaly—the mechanical clockwork scarab device.

If the audience believe that this abnormality is as real as it can be, they will respond to the story. Many directors think that the more you keep the creature in the shadows and don't show it, the better it is, but I don't believe that. I don't have monsters in my movies, I have characters, so I shoot the monsters as characters. For example, in **Hellboy**, I shot Abe Sapien, the fish-man, like any other actor. I didn't fuss about it, I shot the monster with the same conviction that I would shoot Cary Grant or Brad Pitt; in other words, if I shot it in a different way than I would the regular actors, I would be making a mistake.

What I do in every movie very consciously is to ensure that this anomaly is shot two notches above actual reality, so it's weird enough to accommodate the monster, but not too stylistic that it's unrecognizable. For example, everything you see in **Pan's Labyrinth**—the house, the furniture—is fabricated to be slightly more theatrical than it needed to be. The uniforms for the captain and his guards are exactly what were worn at the time, but we tweaked the cut and the collar to make them more theatrical. Everything around the creatures, therefore, exists like a terrarium for them to live in so that when it comes to shoot them, I can shoot them in a normal way.

I was very nervous on **Cronos**, but the adrenaline carried me through. Directing is almost like keeping four balls in the air on a monocycle with a train approaching behind you. There were days, for example, like the scene with the husband sleeping under the bed, where I knew I'd fucked up. The makeup was wrong and we didn't have time to go back and change it, we didn't even have time to test it. The light was wrong. Everything was wrong, and I arrived home to my wife that night and cried. I said that I had destroyed the scene I had dreamt of for years. I didn't have the luxury of reshoots. Of course, you can only break down in front of →

CRONOS

(01–02) After the release of **Cronos**, Del Toro met Pedro Almodóvar at the Miami International Film Festival and Almodóvar told him how much he loved the film. "He said it doesn't look like a first movie and he said he would love to produce any movie I ever wanted to make in Spain," recalls Del Toro. "That was how [Pedro and his brother Agustín Almodóvar] ended up producing **The Devil's Backbone**. It was also delicate because I wanted to cast Marisa Paredes and I wanted his blessing for that. He said 'Absolutely, she's right for the part.'"

THE DEVIL'S BACKBONE / PAN'S LABYRINTH

(01–05) Del Toro says that for many audiences, **Pan's Labyrinth** was the first film for which he was recognized as a filmmaker. But for him, that happened with **The Devil's Backbone** five years earlier. "I always say that **The Devil's Backbone** is my first film and it remains my favorite. For most people **Pan's Labyrinth** was the movie they got to see me through. Ironically, **Pan's Labyrinth** was a really difficult experience for me, and it is a close second to **Mimic** (1997) as the hardest film to make. It was a very personal film and we didn't have the budget. We had great support from some people, but also a lot of enemies who didn't want it to happen, and ultimately the movie was a declaration of principle. I was making the movie to say 'This is the way I see the world. I am Ofelia, I was Ofelia as a kid and I am Ofelia as a filmmaker.' At the end, when it says that the only thing she left behind were little traces of herself in the world for those who know where to look, that's how I feel about my movies: little things that you really look for, you take notice. I am not a brand name, I am an acquired taste and I really love being an acquired taste."

For all its sense of wonder, **Pan's Labyrinth** also included three shocking scenes of violence carried out by Vidal (Sergi López), which caused some of the film's backers to balk. "I was very clear about the violence," he says. "For the movie to work, you had to have all three scenes. Not one of them is gratuitous. The first one shows you this man's character, like Scorsese shows Joe Pesci's character in **Goodfellas** (1990). Once you see Pesci kill his first guy in that film, you go 'Holy Crap' and you are on edge with that guy for the rest of the movie."

Vidal is reminiscent of the villain Jacinto (played by Eduardo Noriega) in **The Devil's Backbone**. "We wanted a very good-looking guy, but if I made him any less angry, the audience would want to forgive him because great-looking people are given a lot of leeway in society, so I wanted a guy that hated himself and was really uncomfortable in his own skin, but was still good looking. If you watch the movie, you can see that Noriega gets uglier and uglier as the film progresses, his nose gets broken, his eye gets all bloodshot until at the end of the movie, he really looks like a monster and the makeup of the ghost gets more and more beatific, he gets to be almost beautiful. It was a reversal in a way."

01 Eduardo Noriega and Irene Visedo in **The Devil's Backbone**

02 The ghost becomes more beautiful as **The Devil's Backbone** progresses

03 Pale Man/Fauno in **Pan's Labyrinth**. As Del Toro says, he shoots "the monsters as characters"

04 Ivana Baquero as Ofelia in **Pan's Labyrinth**

05 Sergi López as Vidal, perhaps the real "monster" in **Pan's Labyrinth**

> "The most salient thing you can gain as a director is experience in transforming adversity into creativity. When you direct, the only thing you can claim as the years go by is that you get better at dealing with the unexpected."

your wife, or your partner, or your parents. In front of the staff on the film, you need to keep total control. You don't want anyone thinking the general is afraid—you have to be leading the charge. There are two very lonely positions on a movie set: the actor and the director. The cinematographer has a close liaison with the director, the gaffer, the grip, etc. The director is alone on one end of the lens and the actor is alone on the other. That's why the great, most satisfying partnerships on set are when a director and actor come to love and support each other.

Being from Mexico is an enormous part of who I am as a filmmaker. The panache, the sense of melodrama, and the madness I have in my movies that allows me to mix historical events with fictional creatures, all comes from an almost surreal Mexican sensibility. I'm really prone to melodrama. This comes from watching Mexican melodrama obsessively, to the point where I was watching **The Devil's Backbone** with a Spanish architect and the architect said to me that it was more Mexico than Spain; the characters were acting like Latin characters. If my father hadn't been kidnapped in 1998 then frankly I would be making Mexican movies interspersed with the European and American. Since 1998, I cannot go

back to Mexico because I would be too visible a target, especially when there is a printed schedule of where I am going to be every day for the entire run of a shoot.

I think of the audience every second during writing; I think of them as me. I question how I would understand something, or what would make me feel a certain way. When I'm shooting a scene that moves the characters, I weep, I feel the emotion on set, so when I am writing it, if it doesn't work, I don't print it out until I have that feeling. Creating tension is a different skill to creating fear. For fear, you try to create atmosphere. You ensure the scene is alive visually before anything is added, then you craft the silence very carefully because silence often equals fear.

Rarely can you elicit fear with music unless the music is used very discreetly, underlining the scene in a way that is almost invisible. When the Pale Man appears in **Pan's Labyrinth** there is music, but Javier [Navarrete, the film's composer] is almost just underlining his movements. It becomes like a sound effect. Silence is one of the things that you learn to craft the most because there is never real silence in a movie; you always have distant wind, cars, dogs barking, or →

MIMIC

(01) Del Toro battled with Miramax Films on the production and final cut of **Mimic**, a film about a growing swarm of giant insects living in the New York subway system. "I think I learned a single word out of **Mimic** and that was the word 'no.' I learned to say no," he says.

"Until then, I had been a guy who worked with friends. In Mexico, if you need help or if a friend of yours needs help, you say yes and when you ask them to help you, they say yes. So you live in a world where mutual dependence assures true collaboration. **Mimic** showed me that it wasn't that way in America. I think failure teaches you a lot." Del Toro's cut was released on DVD last year on the film's 15th anniversary. "It's not exactly as I would have done it if I was left alone, but it's the closest to it," he says. "I like the movie now."

BLADE II

Stephen Norrington had already directed **Blade** when Del Toro was drafted in to make the sequel **Blade II**.

(**02–03**) "I met with [the film's star] Wesley Snipes and told him that I didn't really understand **Blade**," recalls Del Toro. "I told him I'd love to shoot him fighting, but I like the vampires more than the Blade character. I told him 'I would like to make a memorable monster and you can be the hero.' He said that sounded like a great partnership. I really enjoyed working with him."

HELLBOY

(01–03) Although they were made inside the Hollywood studio system, Del Toro says that the two **Hellboy** movies are anything but conventional comic-book movies.

"People should realize to this day what an anomaly the **Hellboy** films are, a huge anomaly," he says. "They are movies that star a red guy, co-starring a fish-man and, if you watch them very carefully, they go against the grain of the action superhero movies in almost every way (**02**). The most flawed character in the films is Hellboy himself. He makes more mistakes than anyone, he is a goof. He screws up constantly. His great advantage is that he is essentially immortal and can take a lot of wear and tear. They are very strange movies."

Again Del Toro worked hard to show the domesticity of the monsters in the film. "His appetites are incredibly human. He loves chili nachos and pancakes. He's not very well read and can't pronounce certain words. He's a guy that you'd love to have a beer with. That domesticity allows the magic to feel more real."

Collaborations

One of Del Toro's closest collaborators is cinematographer Guillermo Navarro, who has shot every film except **Mimic** and **Blade II**. "After twenty years together, we are like brothers," he says. "I love working with him. It's a very comfortable creative relationship. I know what he does, he knows what I do and we don't try to meddle with each other. The more you work with people you know, the less you have to explain yourself to them. So it's like a great marriage. They know your habits, you don't have to argue about it. I try to work with a lot of people I know."

HELLBOY II: THE GOLDEN ARMY

(04–05) Del Toro says that one of the best scenes he has ever shot is the troll market sequence in **Hellboy II**.

"It's full of rich people," he says. "Every nook and cranny is occupied by a really great monster. It's one of those extravaganzas that are impossible to do anymore and it feels really magical. If you just had a movie with regular people, you could not reach those peaks of extravagance."

For this sequence, Del Toro hired different designers for each creature. "It's like casting actors," he says. "I give them input as they design them, but I let them run with each creature from beginning to end. It's a rare process. Normally the way a movie company goes is they hire the designer who designs the creatures, they hire a makeup company that fabricates the creatures, and they hire a wardrobe department that dresses the creatures. What I do is the opposite. I hire a bunch of guys and they design the creatures, fabricate and dress them, and operate the controls when they are put in front of the camera. I don't think anyone else does it this way," he explains.

"I used to travel with a trunkful of movies. Now I have four little hard drives with 1,850 movies on them, all legally acquired I may add."

crickets in the distance. I think really well-crafted silence creates tension, and by the same token an empty frame, an empty corridor for example—if it's empty in the right, creepy way—is a tool.

You know if a scene's not working on set, and as you get older and craftier, you can learn to re-direct it in post. You can patch it up in your coverage and recover it—you can even end up with a great scene because beauty rarely comes out of perfection. For something to work, I think it has to come out of emotional turmoil. You can't encapsulate the perfect melody; a huge component of it is instinctive.

Then, of course, there are the actors. Many times you storyboard and rehearse with the actor, and then you come to the scene and it's not working. But then you try something different and something suddenly happens that makes it work. It's very raw. It's funny, we enthrone this idea of the perfect filmmaker, this myth of the all-controlling, all-seeing, all-encompassing person, but even for Kubrick or von Stroheim there is a part of the process that is entirely instinctive. I once asked Tom Cruise about it and he confirmed that Kubrick often found things in a panic on **Eyes Wide Shut** (1999).

I love imperfection. I have been friends with James Cameron since 1992 and because he is so incredibly precise, people sometimes don't think he is human, but the beauty of being a close friend is that I've seen him burn the midnight oil and toil and sweat. These imperfections in the façade are what make the work more admirable. Art depends on that human touch that doesn't make perfection; in fact the filmmakers and films I am most attracted to require a level of human imperfection.

On the big effects films, you try to prepare thoroughly but there are always surprises. John Lennon said "Life is what happens when you are making other plans" and I think film is what

Advice to young filmmakers

"If you really want to be a filmmaker, you need to learn to tell stories and the only way to learn to tell stories is by watching a lot of movies and reading a lot of screenplays. Sit down and forget about writing every day, learn how to read film. You need to make yourself truly educated enough if you can and watch at least a couple of the great movies made every year since cinema was invented. Learn about Max Ophüls and Erich von Stroheim, and F. W. Murnau and Carl Theodor Dreyer and find things that they were trying that will illuminate what Scorsese or Nolan is doing. But when you come at film and the oldest thing that you know is twenty years old, that's a problem. I remember talking to a young director and he said he loved old movies like **Taxi Driver** (1976) and I said 'Since when is that an old film?' To have Buster Keaton and Chaplin under your belt is invaluable and I really advise people to watch movies and read movies, and constantly be in love with the medium. And avoid reading the trades or the business stuff. I make it a habit not to read about the business side because that is not filmmaking. I hate the language that has permeated most of the blogs and the fan sites. When I was a fan, you were enraptured discussing Fellini or a long tracking shot or the humanity of Renoir. That was being a cinephile. Nobody that I remember in the 1970s or 1980s was talking about target audiences, tracking, which studio was weaker, or four-quadrant appeal. It's entering the building the wrong way. One of my most cherished rituals when I am shooting is waking up really early and playing 20–30 minutes of one of my favorite movies just to remind me what it is I am doing. I am not dealing with the producer or the production designer or working out how to make up for the fact I am two days behind. That is what really helped me through **Mimic**. I just say: 'This is what I do, this is my craft.'"

> "I don't have monsters in my movies, I have characters, so I shoot the monsters as characters."

happens when you are making other plans. You come onto the set and either the actor or the material doesn't come out as you expect and the film comes out better for it. If you have either experience or inspiration, one of the two will get you through. One you accumulate through the years, the other you cherish.

As a young filmmaker you're full of inspiration and if you are unlucky you are only trading it in for experience. You need to remain on dangerous ground to continue to be inspired. I am always tackling things I shouldn't tackle and meddling with stuff I shouldn't meddle with. You never have enough money. If you ever feel one day you have enough money, that's the day you're fucked. "

01 Del Toro on the set of **Hellboy II: The Golden Army** with Ron Perlman, Selma Blair and Doug Jones

Producing other movies

Del Toro works to nurture and produce the work of other directors, but he says the process is just as rewarding for him. "I argue with the director just to give him a different perspective," he says, "and tell him that at the end of the day it's his choice. But when Juan Antonio Bayona on **The Orphanage** (2007) **(02–03)** goes off and does something a different way than I would do and I see how wonderful it is, I am the one who's learning from the guy and growing as a filmmaker. Of course, I look at their assemblies and give advice. I think we are all better filmmakers when we are watching somebody else's films. It's incredibly easy to say he didn't do this or that, but when you are executing it, you can get lost. That's part of why the most salient thing you can gain as a director is experience in transforming adversity into creativity. When you direct, the only thing you can claim as the years go by is that you get better at dealing with the unexpected."

John Ford

John Ford made his first film in 1914 and, before his death in 1973, he would become arguably the most influential filmmaker to emerge from the US studio system, both inside and out. He has four Oscars to his name for best director, a feat unequalled since his death, and was beloved by some of the world's greats, including Akira Kurosawa, Jean-Luc Godard, Ingmar Bergman and Orson Welles. Some of the greatest American films—namely **Stagecoach** (1939), **The Grapes of Wrath** (1940) and **The Searchers** (1956)—are Ford films.

A populist filmmaker best known for his westerns, he was at his best depicting America's past and spirit with an almost naïve idealism. His images are poetic and he famously placed characters in vast natural landscapes captured in long shots of breathtaking beauty. His storytelling, while simple, was masterful and classic, in the literal sense of the word.

The thirteenth child of an Irish immigrant family, Ford was born in 1894 as John Martin Feeney and raised in Maine, but left for Hollywood in 1914 where he started work as

01 John Ford

02 The Informer

03 The Searchers

"His images are poetic and he famously placed characters in vast natural landscapes captured in long shots of breathtaking beauty."

a set worker and propman before becoming an assistant director and finally a director. He made countless silent films, including **The Iron Horse** (1924)—about the building of the first transcontinental railroad, which would presage his fascination with the American frontier.

(1941). The last two won him his second and third directing Oscars.

After the war, he made classic after classic including westerns **My Darling Clementine** (1946), **Fort Apache** (1948), **She Wore a Yellow Ribbon** (1949) and **Rio Grande** (1950), and the

Clint Eastwood

"I think I am a good leader. Because I do it with respect and on time, and without a lot of fanfare. I figure you're a good leader if they like what you're doing."

Clint Eastwood was already a box-office superstar in front of the camera when he turned to directing in 1971 with **Play Misty for Me**. And while he maintained his career as a movie star for several decades to come, he achieved his greatest success and acclaim directing over thirty films since then. In the 1970s and early 1980s, he made some iconic westerns such as **High Plains Drifter** (1973) and **The Outlaw Josey Wales** (1976), and action movies like **The Gauntlet** (1977) and **Sudden Impact** (1983), but it was with his Charlie Parker biopic **Bird**, which played in competition at the Cannes Film Festival in 1988, that Eastwood gained a new global respect as a filmmaker. This was sealed in his own country with the Oscars for Best Picture and Best Director four years later for his superb western **Unforgiven** (1992). Since then, he has worked feverishly, delivering an eclectic range of films including **A Perfect World** (1993), **The Bridges of Madison County** (1995), **Midnight in the Garden of Good and Evil** (1997), and **Space Cowboys** (2000). He developed a reputation for brisk, efficient filmmaking and measured, uncluttered mise-en-scène.

It was in the early part of the 21st century, in his seventies, that Eastwood appeared to hit a golden period starting with **Mystic River**, a multiple Oscar winner in 2003, followed a year later by **Million Dollar Baby**, which won Eastwood the Best Picture/Director Oscar double once again. In 2006, he delivered two films on the subject of the battle for Iwo Jima—**Flags of Our Fathers** and **Letters from Iwo Jima**. Two more films followed in 2008—**Changeling** and box-office smash **Gran Torino**. His latest film is **J. Edgar** starring Leonardo DiCaprio and Armie Hammer.

Clint Eastwood

" Over the years when I was an actor, I became interested in working with actors and found different atmospheres that I liked with different directors that made acting more compatible. The sets didn't have to be nerve-wracking or bell-ringing or booby-trapped as it was with some. I started developing my own theories on it and incorporated all my experience into them. A lifetime in movies is the same as a lifetime in any profession: you are constantly a student. Every film is different and has different obstacles to overcome and that's what makes it interesting. That's why I continue to do it and enjoy the challenges of it. As long as you remain open to new ideas and developing your own philosophies as you go, it's a very enjoyable process.

I took from everyone I worked with of course—from Sergio Leone and Don Siegel, and all the directors on the TV series **Rawhide** (1959–66). You see different people approaching things differently and you can tell when they have a certain amount of knowledge or when they're faking it. Subconsciously I think you take from everybody. Sometimes when I am doing a scene, I try to think how so-and-so did it in that 1936 film. Or you remember seeing some effect as a kid and try to get the same effect. As an American kid growing up, watching Howard Hawks or John Ford or Alfred Hitchcock or Billy Wilder, you watched their work and it was amazing how they created certain excitement in their films.

When I did **Rawhide**, we had a lot of old-time directors who had stopped doing movies—people like Stuart Heisler and Laszlo Benedek. I had also done three weeks on a movie with William Wellman, and watched everything he did—how he approached things, how people responded to him, how he liked the sets, the atmosphere. I found out what he liked actors to do and what he didn't like.

For me, it's very important to have a comfortable and calm environment on set. It's important that the actors are submerging themselves into the character to the greatest

Making music

Eastwood is that rare director who also writes much of the music for his films, and is famous for his sparing jazz-inflected scores. "I don't always use myself," he says. "Sometimes other people come in. Certainly other composers out there have a lot more experience than me, but sometimes it's hard to explain to them what I want and I just do it myself. On **Mystic River** (**01**), I had a certain idea and went over to a friend of mine's studio and designed the main theme and then added instruments to it. On **Million Dollar Baby**, I wrote the theme to it and we switched stuff and overdubbed. Sometimes in the past, I've had composers come in that are terrific and can enhance everything you're doing and sometimes they never quite get the same idea you are trying to transmit. It's not their fault, maybe it's just a question of me not explaining it well or them seeing a moment where the music is more dynamic than it should be and you get a score that overrides the film. I like the score to be supportive of the film."

01

degree and the best way to do that is to give them full confidence and ensure they don't feel like they're riding a ship that's on the brink of disaster.

Sometimes I rehearse with the actors, sometimes I don't. Most actors have a pretty good idea coming to it, because it's what attracted them to the role. Some are extremely instinctive and grasp the character right on. A great example of that would be Gene Hackman in **Unforgiven**. He had the character so perfect right out of the box on every shot, every sequence, and he really didn't have to do anything different—he was amazing. Sometimes when I'm rehearsing for a camera move, the performance is so good that I just turn the camera on, not wanting to lose it. I've seen it happen in the past that actors come out really good at the start and then all of a sudden, they start killing it with improvements.

Sometimes there are actors who can drift in and jump in and out more easily. As a director, you have one relationship with them. Others need to stay in character and you have another relationship with them.

I remember when we were doing **Rawhide** on soundstages, people would use megaphones to get everybody quiet and the more people yelled "Quiet," the louder the extras would yell and nothing was quiet. I realized that actors need a little bit of time to think, not feel pressured about the whole thing, because not all of them are extroverted people who can't wait to clown around in front of a camera. They want to stay there and get into a role, and I want to keep them there as long as they want to be there.

I have a reputation for always going with the first or second take. Of course, I don't always get it in one or two takes. It's more that I want to get the feeling that we're moving. You have to keep the crew and the production going at a business-like pace so they get the feeling they are part of something that's actually moving forward.

The cast and crew feel like they are going somewhere when they go to work each day and feel like they are accomplishing something →

02

CHANGELING

(01–03) This film is memorable, among other things, for its authentic depiction of Los Angeles in the late 1920s and early 1930s, but Eastwood didn't have to go further than his own memories to verify its authenticity. "I lived in Los Angeles in the early thirties for a while and although I was a very young boy, I know exactly what the roads looked like, and the atmosphere of the place. I have vivid memories of it. It was much more rural than it is now in the outskirts, and the film took place in the outskirts, in Riverside. In those days, it would have taken all day to drive where you were going on the bad roads."

and not just doing the same scene each day. I like to do whole sequences in one day, so everyone has the feeling that all the parts are there and, besides, it helps for editing purposes. It's my job to make sure that the set and atmosphere that everyone is working in is comfortable. That's the way to get the best out of people.

Sometimes I don't change a good script at all. I bought the **Unforgiven** script in 1980 and put it in a drawer and said I'll do this some day—it's good material and I'll rewrite it. And I took it from the drawer ten years later and called up the writer and said I had a couple of ideas and wanted to rewrite some of it, and he was fine with that. I told him I might call him because I wanted him to approve my changes. So I went to work and the more I tooled with it, the more I realized I was killing it with improvements. So I went back to him and said that I had been working on these ideas and I really felt I was wrecking it, so I was just going to go with it the way it was. So I did. Of course, you make improvements along the way, but generally when you start intellectualizing it, you can take the spirit out of it.

On other occasions, you get a script where the idea is terrific, but the execution isn't quite right or doesn't suit the actors that you're hiring, so you adapt it and add things to it. I've made changes to everything I've done, but with some of them it's a minor knick-knack here and there, and on others you rework it entirely from the start.

During shooting, I have certain objectives, but I am never locked into things. In other words, when I am going on a location, I don't say it has to be this way because this is the way we looked at it two months ago so this is the way it has to be.

I'm always flexible, I always improvise. If we looked at the location in the fall and the sun in the summer makes it a different place, I change it. If an actor is left-handed instead of right-handed, I ask them to come in whichever direction is more natural to them. I am using simplistic analysis here, but there is no rule that has to be stuck to rigidly.

Likewise, I am flexible with the script during production. Sometimes I get an idea in one scene that will stimulate something else. Or I'd like to see the actors do that, or maybe this character would do that.

I always like to feel I am doing something different on every picture. If I'm not, if I feel like I am doing something reminiscent of a lot of things I've done before, it would cause me anxiety that I was repeating myself. That's why after **Unforgiven**, I thought that was a perfect time for me to stop doing the western. Not for anybody else, but I would hate to be doing the same genre continually. That's why I left Italy, because after doing three movies with Sergio Leone I felt I had done as much as I could with that character and I thought it was time for me to go home and get other ideas.

When I did **Bird**, it was a surprise to some people, first because I wasn't in it and second because most of the films I'd been doing were cop movies or westerns or adventure films, so to be doing one about Charlie Parker, who was a great influence on American music, was a great thrill for me.

But whether it's a drama or an action film, the story content is everything to me. Sometimes it's good and sometimes not, and that is in the eye of the beholder. You definitely have to step up to the bat and try to hit the ball out of the park. If you don't, you should at least try to be innovative, and hopefully the audience will respond to that.

I always think about the audience. When you are thinking about telling the story, you are thinking about how you want the story to be as interesting as it possibly can be for the audience—otherwise it will never take on the life it's supposed to have out there with the audience.

It's hard to be a judge of that. You can't start thinking about it too much because a lot of wonderful movies haven't done any business and a lot of not-so-wonderful movies have done tremendous business. All you can do is use yourself as the audience, ask yourself if you were going to the theater how would you like to see this. What about this actor in that part? In every element of the film, there's always that thing an audience is going to see and judge, like or dislike. Of course, once you have committed yourself to doing it on a film, that's it. If the audience likes it, that's great; if it doesn't, go back to the drawingboard for the next feature.

I can work quite fast. If the next project is there and it's good and it's something that's been brewing for a while, I can move onto it. If it's not there, then I won't. For example, when I was doing post-production and editing on **Mystic River**, I read **Million Dollar Baby**. I had read the book it came from some years earlier and liked the script and I thought "Well, I'll do this." And they asked when I wanted to do it and I said "well, right away." We ended up getting Morgan Freeman and Hilary Swank, and we just went ahead and started doing it. One went right →

LETTERS FROM IWO JIMA / FLAGS OF OUR FATHERS

(01–08) Eastwood's capacity to adapt when he is shooting is evident in the creation of **Letters from Iwo Jima**, a film that evolved while he was shooting **Flags of Our Fathers**, a story about US soldiers in the battle for Iwo Jima and at home afterwards. "In the execution of [**Flags of Our Fathers**], I started reading about the other side and in particular General Kuribayashi," he explains. "The whole idea was very difficult for Americans to understand, that sense of soldiers being told you are never coming back, that you are going to stay there and defend it until you are dead. That is a very hard sell for Americans, so I wondered what it was like for a guy like Kuribayashi who was well-educated, had gone to Harvard for a while, had learned English and American customs, and traveled a lot to our country. What was it like for him to be back fighting against people that he had been friends with at some point in his life. And what was it like for a group of young boys between 15 and 25 who were conscripts in the military being sent to an island to their deaths. These thoughts gave me the curiosity to go back and call a friend of mine in Japan and ask if there were any books on this man. It started from there and eventually we came up with a script. It started from scratch."

01–04 Letters from Iwo Jima

02 Ken Watanabe as General
Kuribayashi in **Letters from Iwo Jima**

05–08 Flags of Our Fathers

"I used to work with Henry Bumstead until just before he passed away aged 92. He had seen more than I had ever seen on the planet and knew exactly what I was talking about and he used to get mad at me and say 'Clint, you should be hiring a younger production designer,' and I'd say 'No, I need your wisdom. And also, you're older than me and I don't want to be the oldest guy on the set.'"

MILLION DOLLAR BABY

(01–03) Eastwood doesn't go into deep research on all his films. When he read the script for **Million Dollar Baby**, for example, he felt comfortable that he could produce a convincing onscreen picture of the female boxing world based on conversations in his past. "Actually, I had done a lot of action movies with a lot of fight sequences and I used to train with a great fight trainer years ago myself called Al Silvani. I knew a girl once who became a female boxer around the casinos in Vegas and I sent over Al, who trained Rocky Graziano among others, and said let's see if he can add anything to your education. When he came back, he said she was great. So when **Million Dollar Baby** came up, I felt I had a small familiarity with that and I just approached it from that standpoint. I hadn't seen a girl fight or any female boxing before. I just knew of them and figured how it would be." The film won Eastwood Best Picture and Best Director Oscars in 2005, and both Hilary Swank and Morgan Freeman also received Oscars for their performances in the film.

01

Advice for young directors

"I would say use everything you've ever learned in life and everything you've ever seen and incorporate it all. And don't let people talk you out of a strong idea on something. Be aware that there are pitfalls and that people want to make you aware of the pitfalls, but don't give up on the idea if it's a good one. You have to believe in yourself, believe that you can do it and just go out and do it. You don't want to ponder something to the point where you get indecisive, and people can do that because there's always a million reasons why something won't work, but you have to say well there's also a million reasons why it might work, so let's go do it."

04   Gran Torino

> "I always think about the audience. When you are thinking about telling the story, you are thinking about how you want the story to be as interesting as it possibly can be for the audience."

behind the other, but it doesn't always happen like that. Sometimes you have to wait for a while for a very good script to come and I don't make films just to be working. I might have done that when I was younger, but now it has to be something that I have a certain feeling for.

I am never looking for anything specific. With **J. Edgar**, I read the script and found it interesting and said I would like to do it. It's not like I was longing to do something on J. Edgar Hoover, although I had grown up on J. Edgar Hoover as a little boy. Everyone knew about him as the head of the FBI and I was always kind of curious about it. And, of course, he was an odd character who people were curious about, so it was interesting to explore a little bit.

I don't always shoot a lot of coverage. I try to shoot just what I want to see and sometimes it doesn't work out that way, because when you get into editing, you realize maybe there's something wrong or there's a redundancy to one scene as it

fits in the puzzle and you forego it. It's the final molding process, like working with a piece of clay and you can break a film in editing by doing it improperly or enhance it with good editing.

My relationship with Warner Bros. helps me. As long as somebody finances you, can make a film and get it seen any place and in any language, then hopefully it's a success. You can always look at it like it's a crapshoot. Either way, it's a lot of good people working hard to tell a story and there are so many people involved. It's really a little army, or a small platoon, and you're going out into the field and trying to make something. You're only as good as your weakest link and I try to get everybody to contribute imaginatively. If somebody has an idea, I don't care what department they are in, I listen to it because people come up with good ideas. And because directors have so much to do, you can stymie yourself by not paying attention to what's around you.

HEREAFTER

(01–02) Eastwood's 2010 drama **Hereafter** opens with a spectacularly authentic and horrifying CGI recreation of the 2004 tsunami in Southeast Asia. He shot the sequences with actress Cécile de France and others over four days, but the real work came in post-production. "I had worked with [visual effects supervisor] Michael Owens on **Space Cowboys** and so I called him up and said we wanted to do the tsunami sequence," recalls Eastwood. "So we all sat down and started looking at various amateur footage of the horrific tsunami. We devised a story of what would happen to the character—where she would go, how she would be thrown about and where she would end up. We laid it out, went over to Lahaina on the island of Maui and shot there, then did some water-tank work in London. Michael and his people had to know where all the other [CGI] stuff was going to be. The biggest trick we achieved was to make it take place from the inside, so you were following the character struggling to stay alive while the world is coming apart around her."

01

02

Collaborating with the same people and creating a shorthand

Eastwood has worked with a group of the same collaborators and department heads over many of his films. His current troupe includes producer Robert Lorenz, cinematographer Tom Stern (03), editor Joel Cox, and production designer James T. Murakami.

"I work with a lot of the same collaborators and you develop a great shorthand," he says. "You don't have to sit there and explain from scratch what you want. You can just say I want this like Monet or you want the look they had in this movie from 1938, even if that movie is black and white and you are shooting in color. And everybody understands. I used to work with [production designer] Henry Bumstead until just before he passed away aged 92. He had seen more than I had ever seen on the planet and knew exactly what I was talking about and he used

to get mad at me and say 'Clint, you should be hiring a younger production designer,' and I'd say 'No, I need your wisdom. And also, you're older than me and I don't want to be the oldest guy on the set.' Tom Stern has been with me for a lot of years: he was a gaffer for Bruce Surtees and Jack Green and everybody I've ever used along the way in some way, shape or form. Tom called me one day and said that he thought he could get into the [cinematographers'] guild as a cameraman and it just so happened that I hadn't hired a cameraman yet [on **Blood Work** in 2002], so I hired him. He got in the guild and we started up and I couldn't be more pleased."

03 Cinematographer Tom Stern with Eastwood and Morgan Freeman on the set of **Million Dollar Baby**

Stephen Frears

"I'm told I am unusual in this practice of involving writers, but I am bewildered by those directors who don't. I think you are more in control if you have the writer there because you can say that something isn't working."

Stephen Frears started his career as an assistant on iconic British films in the 1960s such as **Morgan: A Suitable Case for Treatment** (1966), **Charlie Bubbles** (1967), and **If…** (1968), but he cut his teeth directing on television, working with top writers such as Alan Bennett, Tom Stoppard and Christopher Hampton.

He made his feature debut in 1971 with **Gumshoe**, starring Albert Finney as a Liverpool private eye, but has continued to work making outstanding films for TV throughout his career, including **Walter** (1982), **Saigon: Year of the Cat** (1983), and **The Deal** (2003). He also directed a live US TV special of **Fail Safe** in 2000 starring George Clooney.

His theatrical feature career has been distinguished and takes in some of the most celebrated British films of the 1980s, such as **The Hit** (1984), **My Beautiful Laundrette** (1985), **Prick Up Your Ears** (1987), and **Sammy and Rosie Get Laid** (1987).

Dangerous Liaisons, his 1988 film of Laclos' novel **Les Liaisons Dangereuses**, brought him international acclaim and the film was nominated for a Best Picture Oscar, although Frears himself was not nominated until his next film, **The Grifters** (1990), which was produced by Martin Scorsese.

He has worked on both sides of the Atlantic since then on an eclectic range of films, many of them award winning and acclaimed for their narrative sophistication and superb performances. Among his many credits are **The Snapper** (1993), **High Fidelity** (2000), **Dirty Pretty Things** (2002), **Mrs Henderson Presents** (2005), **The Queen** (2006), for which he received a second Oscar nomination, and **Tamara Drewe** (2010).

His most recent film is **Lay the Favorite** (2012), starring Bruce Willis, Rebecca Hall and Catherine Zeta–Jones.

Stephen Frears

"I didn't want to be a filmmaker as a child, but I saw a lot of films because there wasn't a lot else to do. There were forty cinemas in Leicester where I grew up and I probably went twice a week. Then when I went away to [boarding] school, they would show a film on Saturday afternoon to keep the boys quiet. I saw a lot of Will Hay films—I can still quote from **Ask A Policeman** (1939)—and Marx Brothers, and war films. I was endlessly watching Richard Attenborough limping home and Jack Hawkins going down with the ship.

When I was about sixteen, all these great films like **Room at the Top** (1959) came out, films about the world around me, and when I was at Cambridge, I started watching wonderful European films from France and Sweden, Hungary and Czechoslovakia. I remember seeing **A Blonde in Love** (1965) and couldn't believe what I was seeing. When I came down from Cambridge, I ended up at the Royal Court [Theatre in London] and had always wanted to go there because of the intellectually interesting minds that it attracted. It still hadn't crossed my mind to get into film. I worked with Lindsay Anderson there and then Karel Reisz showed up.

Karel suggested that I come and work on **Morgan**, and I went home after the first day of shooting—which was the first day I had ever been on a film set—without a clue as to what was going on. They literally had to explain the difference between a cameraman and the operator. I was what you'd call an idiot savant, but it's actually quite good to have someone on set asking very wide-eyed questions. Why does that happen? Why doesn't he do that? When you ask questions like a child, it stops everybody taking everything for granted. I tell people to avoid subtlety a lot of the time. Show it, make it clear.

I worked with Lindsay Anderson on **If...** and Albert Finney on **Charlie Bubbles**. In my early twenties, I was like a parcel that got passed around between these brilliant men. With Finney, it was his first time directing, so it was like he went to school and I went to school with him. The cameraman was Peter Suschitzky, so he and the other people on the film would explain everything to Albert, and I sat at their feet. I was given a series of lessons. In the end, of course, you only learn how to make films by making them.

In some respects, a director has a narrow, quite subtle job to do. He does the thinking. Everybody else is too busy and concentrating on other things. **Dangerous Liaisons** was a huge jump for me. I was bewildered by 1880s' life in France. They'd show me all these pictures and take me around a chateau, and I hadn't a clue what was going on. In the end, the production designer Stuart Craig, who is a brilliant man, came to me and just laid the film out. He told me that this character was the richest so we'll give her the biggest house. He built corridors past bedrooms and very practical things to realize the physical landscape of the film. It was just brilliant. You just go along with it.

The costume department had a bigger budget than the design budget; they both won Oscars, but Stuart really had nothing to work with and created that out of nothing. It's the illusion of movies.

My first film was a short called **The Burning** (1968). Shorts meant more in those days and mine got played in the cinemas. Nowadays they have become a way for people to avoid making films. The short was set in South Africa on the day the revolution breaks out and it was based on a really good short story. In retrospect, I can see things that I did that I do now. I got a very good crew to shoot it and they got me through because I didn't know what to do.

The short got me jobs, a documentary and a series of children's films for television. I think only when I got to **My Beautiful Laundrette** did I learn to think about audiences, because before that I never had any contact with the audience, even though one of my TV films **Last Summer** (1977) got an audience of 18 million. Television was the most extraordinary nursery for a bunch of us. We had this great subject of post-war Britain and all of us were learning as we did it.

At the end of the day, film or TV, I am just

interested in the material. When I was at Yorkshire Television, I met Neville Smith and we were both out of work so I suggested we do a thriller. Neville sat down and wrote the first forty pages of **Gumshoe** and it was brilliant. I didn't know Neville was brilliant when I met him, or I didn't know what brilliance was, but I suppose I read a really good script and said it was good. I don't know if that means I'm talented.

On **My Beautiful Laundrette**, I think we were incredibly innocent, but we got it made and afterwards you discover it's great and you can't believe your good fortune. When things go right, like when things went right on **The Queen**, I could identify that everything went right, but I had no idea they were part of the mix. If any one of them had gone wrong, we'd have been fucked but they didn't.

Of course, it's depressing when it goes wrong. It's like a train and you can't stop it. You know it's wrong, but there's nothing you can do. You get caught in a machine. On **Mary Reilly** (1996), for example, I knew that we were standing in the wrong place. Christopher [Hampton] originally wrote it for Tim Burton and when he couldn't do it, they came to me. When you make it for a studio, you have to make it on a certain scale. If we had made it for the BBC, it would have been very good. In other words, whatever it is I did →

01 Daniel Day-Lewis and Gordon Warnecke in **My Beautiful Laundrette**

FAIL SAFE

(**02**) In 2000 Frears was approached by George Clooney to direct a live TV version of the 1964 movie **Fail Safe** written by Walter Bernstein. "I had never done anything live before, so I did it because I was curious to see how you did it and if I could do it," he says. "There were long rehearsals and then we had twelve days in the studio. I used to say to [Clooney], why can't we record it and then I'll edit it and we'll say it's live, but he was very shocked by that, so we did it live. It wasn't like the old live TV plays where actors would act out these long scenes. This was entirely based on montage, so what we were really doing in the studio was sharpening the montage all the time. I brought in [celebrated editor] Anne V. Coates to help on what we should show. It was very good fun."

DANGEROUS LIAISONS

(01–04) Still one of Frears' most successful and satisfying films, **Dangerous Liaisons** was the film version of Christopher Hampton's hit stage play, itself adapted from the classic book of letters by Choderlos de Laclos. The film beat another high pedigree version of the story—by the double Oscar winner Milos Forman—to screens and remains the preferred film of the story.

"Sometimes I see bits of it on television and I cannot believe I was allowed near it, but they couldn't get anyone to direct it because Milos was doing the other version," says Frears. "**My Beautiful Laundrette** had been a success, but I was thought to make these rather scruffy, anti-establishment films and in its own way this film is that too."

Frears says he thought of the film as film noir and was thrilled that Warner Bros. was the distributor because the Warner logo was so associated with gangster noir movies in the 1930s. "What I didn't want to do was make something that might be misconstrued as art," he said.

"I was very conscious of Hitchcock and other directors who made dark films when I was making it," he says. "There is a wonderful shot on the staircase when Glenn Close is walking down, telling John Malkovich the story of a man that was beyond her control. I remembered Hitchcock had designed the staircase in **Notorious** (1946) so that it had very wide steps and very flat plane. We were in a chateau, which didn't have a staircase like that, so in the end, John is holding Glenn and bringing her down in a gliding motion to get that effect."

The film begins with a four-minute sequence in which all the characters are shown dressing—a sequence in which Frears and his editor Mick Audsley essentially set up the central conflicts in the film. "I can't say any of it was on my mind when we shot it, but I can see the shots that led to it," says Frears, with typical modesty. "My priority is how to set up the conflict as soon as possible. How soon can we get there? How little do we have to do to get there?"

"Having the nerve to say that something is dull is important. You're not saying it critically, you are saying that together we have come up with something rather dull, so why can't we come up with something interesting? Obviously you learn as you go on."

was completely inappropriate for it, so you really are in charge of a runaway horse. I stopped it once because I knew it was a mistake, but then Julia Roberts came on board and she was terrific, and she put the price up so you become helpless. I won't watch it now.

I tend to think I know before everybody else that something's going wrong. I can remember **The Snapper** (1993), which was a wonderful experience and when we made **The Van** (1996), I shot a scene and I thought I ought to be feeling something, why am I not feeling something? Well I should have been feeling something if I got the film right. It's intuitive.

Then again, I can't explain why **Dangerous Liaisons** went so right. We got it right, all down the line. At the time, Christopher Hampton thought I'd gone mad when I cast Keanu Reeves. He thought I'd lost my senses. But it worked.

The writers tend to be my friends and they are always on set. I scarcely shoot without them there. I don't understand why you wouldn't. You have a cameraman, you have a grip, you have a sound recordist, you should have a writer there. It's just part of the same process. On **Lay the Favorite**, D.V. DeVicentis, who wrote **High Fidelity** as well, was a producer so it was a way of him being there the whole time. He did an enormous amount of work during production: he was rewriting the whole time. Even in the cutting room, we are still rewriting, filleting bits out. I'm told I am unusual in this practice of involving writers, but I am bewildered by those directors who don't. I think you are more in control if you have the writer there because you can say that something isn't working. Moira Buffini on **Tamara Drewe** was rewriting scenes all the time. She was like an American gag writer.

Hanif Kureishi on **My Beautiful Laundrette** was making things up all the time, like the bloke on the phone in the laundrette, which was completely improvised on set.

I am not a shouter. If you have to shout, there is something wrong. You have to be able to win every argument, not in order to satisfy yourself, but for the right reasons. Your thinking has to

be absolutely right and if you can't win the argument, something is wrong with your thinking.

You need to be able to convince everybody. I was doing a scene on **Lay the Favorite**, the day was getting behind and everything was going wrong. When we finally decided on where to shoot the scene, Bruce [Willis] started playing it in a rather dramatic way and eventually I cleared my head and said that I always thought of the scene as a sort of a joke, so we should shoot it with one camera and do it in a two shot. Then he understood. Luckily I was able to clear my head: that's the bit you have to get right. In spite of everyone pulling you in the wrong way, you have to have the presence of mind to say it isn't that, it's that. And everybody has to realize that you are right.

I always tell the actors to do it fast. I remember seeing Gary Oldman when he was cutting **Nil by Mouth** (1997) and he told me that when we were doing **Prick Up Your Ears** (1987), he and Alfred Molina used to laugh because I would always tell them to go faster. Now he was sitting looking at his movie some years later and wishing that he had made his actors go faster. Billy Wilder used to put a stopwatch on them, and I remember Richard Dreyfuss saying that Spielberg would say "That was a very good 58-second shoot of the scene, now do it in 45."

You learn it over the years. I read that Frank Capra would record the audience watching one of his films and he discovered that an audience thinks faster than an individual, which was a very profound discovery.

It's not what you expect. On [**Lay the Favorite**], I got the actors to do it very fast and there is no evidence in the cut that they had been told to do it fast at all. They are doing it fast because I told them to, but there is no evidence that they are rushing.

Of course, you need to keep it interesting. I remember that every now and then when we were shooting, [cinematographer] Chris Menges would come up and whisper in my ear "this is very, very boring," and once I'd overcome the desire to strangle him, I realized he was →

THE GRIFTERS

(01) Martin Scorsese, in his capacity as a producer, asked Frears to take on a film of Jim Thompson's, **The Grifters**, after he had seen **My Beautiful Laundrette**.

"It seemed to be an extraordinary piece of psychological intelligence for a man to work out why the qualities on display in **My Beautiful Laundrette** were ideally suited to **The Grifters**," says Frears. Frears persuaded Donald E. Westlake to write the screenplay on the grounds that "it was about the women" and took on the project after he completed **Dangerous Liaisons**.

DIRTY PRETTY THINGS

(02–04) Frears and screenwriter Steven Knight created an unusual portrait of London from the point of view of immigrants in **Dirty Pretty Things**, a thriller that revolved around organ trafficking. And Frears says that he worked with Knight to ramp up the pace. "The speed that you take to get to the central conflict is crucial. When I read the script, the heart in the lavatory was on page 30, but when we made the film, it was on page 10."

absolutely right. Having the nerve to say that something is dull is important. You're not saying it critically, you are saying that together we have come up with something rather dull, so why can't we come up with something interesting? Obviously you learn as you go on. When Ford was making two-reelers, he would say that he had invented really good ways of robbing a bank. That's what the game is: it's not about beautiful tracking shots, it's how to rob the bank interestingly.

In fact, Scorsese said that when you go to see my films, they are not about tracking shots, you just fall in with this group of people and have a good and interesting time. "

01 Anjelica Huston in **The Grifters**

02 & **04** Audrey Tautou as Senay Gelik in **Dirty Pretty Things**

03 Frears directing Chiwetel Ejiofor, who played Okwe, in **Dirty Pretty Things**

Casting the right actors

Frears is famous for working with the biggest stars in the business and many have won awards for their work with him: Helen Mirren won the Oscar for Best Actress for **The Queen** (05), Judi Dench was nominated for **Mrs Henderson Presents**, Anjelica Huston (01) and Annette Bening were nominated for **The Grifters**, and Glenn Close and Michelle Pfeiffer (06) were nominated for **Dangerous Liaisons**.

"You cast with your stomach," he says. "To me casting is the pursuit of clarity. Somebody walks into the room and the whole thing makes sense."

Initially he didn't want to cast Anjelica Huston in **The Grifters**, nor in fact, Rebecca Hall to play a southern US girl in **Lay the Favorite** (07). "[Hall's] agent suggested her to me and I said I wanted an American girl," he recalls. "Eventually I let her audition for me and she came into the room and I told her how prejudiced against her I was. She auditioned anyway and she was brilliant. I had spent a year refusing to cast her."

05 Helen Mirren in **The Queen**, a role for which she won the Oscar for Best Actress

06 Michelle Pfeiffer in **Dangerous Liaisons**

07 Bruce Willis and Rebecca Hall in **Lay the Favorite**

Terry Gilliam

"I actually don't describe myself as a film director. I have to be possessed by an idea or a story. If it consumes me, the film makes itself; I'm just the hand that writes, that's all I am."

One of the most imaginative filmmakers at work in the world today, US-born British director Terry Gilliam was a member of legendary comic troupe Monty Python's Flying Circus in the early 1970s, but his main ambition was to direct films.

He co-directed **Monty Python and the Holy Grail** with Terry Jones in 1974 and made his solo-directing debut on **Jabberwocky** in 1977, but he came into his own with a trio of thrilling fantasies that would mark him out as a rare visionary mind—**Time Bandits** (1981), **Brazil** (1985), and **The Adventures of Baron Munchausen** (1988). The films—one about a boy, one about an adult man, and one about an old man—can be seen as a trilogy.

Although the last of those films was famously beset by production problems and budget over-runs, Gilliam went some way to correct the negative image that Hollywood had of him with **The Fisher King** (1991) and **Twelve Monkeys** (1995), two films made in the studio system that were both highly profitable. Since then, his output has been as diverse and colorful as can be expected from Gilliam—an adaptation of Hunter S. Thompson's **Fear and Loathing in Las Vegas** (1998), a lavish comic fairytale **The Brothers Grimm** (2005), a dark fantasy drama **Tideland** (2005), and a fantastical adventure **The Imaginarium of Doctor Parnassus** (2009).

As if inevitable for a man of such grand vision, Gilliam has met with bad luck since the debacle on **The Adventures of Baron Munchausen**: back problems suffered by his leading actor, Jean Rochefort, forced him to abandon **The Man Who Killed Don Quixote** in 1999 (a crisis documented in the film **Lost in La Mancha**), while the death of his star Heath Ledger midway through production in 2008 caused him to reimagine some of **The Imaginarium of Doctor Parnassus** with different actors (Johnny Depp, Colin Farrell, and Jude Law) all taking on the Ledger role. He is currently attempting to remount the Don Quixote project with a new cast.

Terry Gilliam

" I wake up sometimes and I don't know what to do or even what I do. It's like I don't even know where to start. I don't recognize what skills I have or if I have anything worth saying. I suppose I just start: I jump off the edge of the cliff and see what happens. I knew how to direct films when I began. It's been an unlearning process since then.

I was always into movies. I was 12 when my family moved out to California and we lived in the San Fernando Valley with Hollywood just over the hill. I knew people whose parents were in the film business so it was always there but strangely unattainable.

When I was 23, I took a film-school night course in New York, but lasted only four nights when I realized I wouldn't be getting my hands on any filmmaking equipment. So I read a book on film technique by Eisenstein, and then begged my way into a non-paid job at a stop-motion animation studio. I would sweep up, do any old shit just to be around the activity, watching. From that connection I got a job—again working for free—on a low-budget film of **Finnegans Wake** and I remember there was this one day when they were setting up a shot in a bar around a table and couldn't make it work. I've always had a good spatial sense and quickly realized that they had to have the table on a turntable, but they wouldn't listen so I walked off the film. To me it was obvious what was wrong.

I have always been strong visually, so I understand spatial relationships. I can see the map of something within it. My day job was as Assistant Editor of a humor magazine called **Help!** We featured photographic comic strips called "fumetti"—they are like films without movement. We'd write satirical stories and go out and shoot them. We needed actors, locations, costumes, sets and I was in charge of getting all these things together, so I was learning about the practical aspects of what goes into a film even while editing a magazine.

Despite the fact that I was earning two dollars a week less than what I would have received on the dole, I managed to save enough money to buy my first 16mm Bolex camera. I also bought a little tape recorder. I shared a flat with two other guys—one was a writer, the other a cartoonist—and on weekends, we would buy a three-minute roll of film and, depending on the weather, we'd write a little movie and put on funny clothes and run around. We were inspired by Richard Lester's **The Running, Jumping, Standing Still Film**. We would also roam around post-production houses scavenging discarded rolls of blank film and draw directly onto the film. My first attempt at animation. Everything we did were experiments in storytelling.

All my attempts at filmmaking were put on hold when I came to England working as an illustrator and magazine art director. But I started doing cutout animation for television and soon **Monty Python's Flying Circus** was born. Terry Jones and I were always chaffing at the bit, frustrated with the way the Python shows were lit or shot, so when **Monty Python and the Holy Grail** was given the green light, the two of us leapt, finally getting our chance to direct. We learned on the job.

Terry and I felt that we saw the world the same way and throughout the pre-production and location-scouting process everything went fine. However, when we started shooting, it became clear that we didn't see things as identically as originally thought. I, being the animator and at that time, unable to express myself calmly and patiently, sometimes found it difficult to communicate with the others and it was clear that Terry and I were often saying conflicting things—two different directing voices. So we divided our labor—Terry dealt with the other Pythons while I stayed back with the camera and concentrated on the visual side, the sets and costumes. It worked out well.

I suppose with all of my films after that, I was able to create my own world. Every director is playing God to some extent. And I believe strongly that you have to be true to your creation. You have to protect it. For example: the end of **Brazil**. The studio wanted a happy ending, but that would have made a lie of the world we created. The

MONTY PYTHON AND THE HOLY GRAIL

(01–03) Gilliam and his co-director Terry Jones worked hard on this film to set the comedy within "a very real, smelly, tactile world." Gilliam explains: "It was funnier because it was in a real world. We were inspired by Pasolini films because you could smell them, touch them, feel them and I loved that. We wanted to create the same sense of reality. Some of the scenes like the 'Bring out your dead' scene work fantastically well. I mean [Michael Palin] is eating mud! Despite the fact it was utterly silly, we were doing it with a straight face and in a world that I believed in on every level."

rules of that world were vital, you can't break them just to allow the hero to live happily ever after. In the end Sam Lowry goes mad—he's safe in his own imagination—as happy an ending as allowed in the situation he found himself trapped in.

I think **Blade Runner** was very responsible for my fight with the studio over the ending of **Brazil**; I felt so betrayed by the ending of Ridley's impressive film. My battle for **Brazil** was simply being true to the story and world we had created. Truthfulness is essential.

I'm proud of how we dealt with the limitations of the budget for **Brazil** and created the sense of

a world much richer than what was visible on screen: using posters like "Happiness: we're all in this together." They were essential in implying the existence of the rest of the world because, as in all of my films, there is nothing beyond the edge of the frame. I use every inch. Our ambitions are invariably greater than our budgets. We're never able to afford anything more than what you see. Every detail becomes important—costumes, chairs etc. I get a bit obsessive about that, but it keeps me occupied because, given too much free time, I would rethink everything. I lose confidence quickly, so need to be busy →

focusing on a book or a lampshade in the shot. I have more confidence in the actors because if the casting and script are solid, they'll get through it fine.

I actually don't describe myself as a film director. I have to be possessed by an idea or a story. If it consumes me, the film makes itself; I'm just the hand that writes, that's all I am.

I surround myself by outspoken people, like my director of photography, Nicola Pecorini, who has been with me since **Fear and Loathing in Las Vegas**. Before him was Roger Pratt. They are people who speak their minds and that's what I like. We can argue openly. I want people to have opinions. When I made **The Fisher King**, which was my first film in the US, I was irritated by the hierarchical, fascistic approach to filmmaking where the crew happily took orders without question. It took me weeks to get them involved. British crews are loudmouthed and opinionated. I prefer that.

My approach to the directing business was to learn everybody's job. I have to be able to do every job. I won't do them as well as those hired to do so can, but I have to be able to do them, so that if anybody drops out, we can keep shooting. As directors, you don't get to watch other directors very often unless you hang out on their sets, so it's only by talking to crew people that you understand what it's like to work with Spielberg or Lucas. And what I found out is that I am one of the few guys who seems to understand what everybody's job is, so when I ask somebody to do something, I know it may be difficult or complicated, but not crazy.

When it comes to painting or plastering, and I am telling the painters or plasterers what to do, I can be really annoying. But they appreciate it as well because they realize the director is actually aware of their contribution and can talk to them about it. I may be demanding, but the crews know that I understand and appreciate what they achieve.

My dad was a carpenter and I worked on building sites when I was young. If you come from that background, understanding the making of things, it helps. Similarly, my wife was a

01 Time Bandits

makeup artist for the BBC originally and when we were making **Jabberwocky**, we would sit at home working together on the ogre's teeth. So I know about makeup.

I learned how to talk to actors on **Jabberwocky**. Max Wall and John Le Mesurier believed the credit that stated I was the film director and so they paid attention. They did what I asked them. I thought, how extraordinary. As long as they believe I'm a director and I don't make a fool of myself, we're going to be OK. It was such a relief after **Monty Python**!

I didn't co-direct **Life of Brian** because it had been such a pleasant change working on **Jabberwocky** with actors who would do whatever was asked of them without complaint.

Actors vary. Some want to be told and others want to tell you. I try to only work with people that are going to be fun to work with and are good at their job, so I've become very careful when casting and very conscious of who is going to go on these mountain-climbing expeditions with us. I'm told I am very good with actors, but critics hadn't seemed to notice that before **The Fisher King**. The previous films had so many things to distract them visually and public battles to write about, but **The Fisher King** was much simpler. Just actors acting.

I always looked up to directors like Bergman and said God what must it be like to be able to direct actors? Little by little, I've discovered if →

FEAR AND LOATHING IN LAS VEGAS

(02–05) Alex Cox was originally lined up to direct this film, but when he was dropped, Gilliam stepped in. "Johnny and Benicio were already cast and I had always wanted to work with Johnny, so I took the project on even though I was terrified of it because it was a very important book in my life. So [screenwriter] Tony Grisoni and I threw away Cox's script and produced a new one in eight days (with rewrites, ten days). The idea was very simple: we decided that Duke and Gonzo were Virgil and Dante going to Hell; Virgil is a pagan and, in a sense, so is Gonzo, who is completely amoral. Duke will be the guy with the moral compass that Gonzo eventually goes beyond. I kept saying to everyone that we were sharks, we can only move forward, we can't rest." Gilliam brought in a new, young director of photography, Nicola Pecorini, for the film. "He was my Gonzo and I was Duke, and we just went for it. It was a joy doing that film, never being able to look back or hesitate. Gonzo filmmaking. Just keep going forward and when in doubt, keep shooting."

<u>02</u> Gilliam on location filming
Fear and Loathing in Las Vegas

Film actors

Gilliam's work has featured some of the biggest movie stars of our time including, Sean Connery, Robert De Niro, Robin Williams, Bruce Willis, Johnny Depp, Matt Damon, Jeff Bridges, Brad Pitt, Heath Ledger, and Benicio Del Toro.

"Some of these guys, like Jeff [Bridges] and Johnny [Depp], really understand exactly where the film frame is," he says. "There is a scene in **Fear and Loathing in Las Vegas** when Johnny and Benicio are in the car driving with Tobey Maguire in the back seat and we were using a wide-angle lens, and Johnny is talking right into camera while moving his cigarette holder to mark the corners of the frame (05). Just for the fun of it. It was extraordinary. Johnny has a Zen-like sense of the frame that is so precise that he can hit a mark he can't see from ten meters away."

Wide angles

Gilliam became famous, especially in **Brazil** (03–06), for his use of wide-angle lenses to lend a hallucinatory, surreal quality to his images.

"Because they incorporate more than your peripheral vision you are seeing an awful lot and interiors become claustrophobic," he explains. "I am always obsessed about the world that people live in as much as the characters. I thought that a long lens was cheating because it isolates the thing you want the audience to focus on rather than keeping it an integral part of the world. A wide-angle lens shows everything in focus—the guy in the background as well as the main character. They are all important to me. When I was looking through the camera I wanted to climb inside the world we were photographing. The wide-angle lens allowed me. They are slower to work with because it is more difficult to hide the lights and they can create problems like distortion. The distance between the actor and the lens becomes critical because otherwise it distorts too much. Jonathan Pryce was often very close to the camera in **Brazil** and sometimes that worked well, like when he is in the padded cell at the end. But sometimes it was very complicated and time-consuming to get the set-ups right."

01–02 Pages from Gilliam's original storyboards for **Brazil**

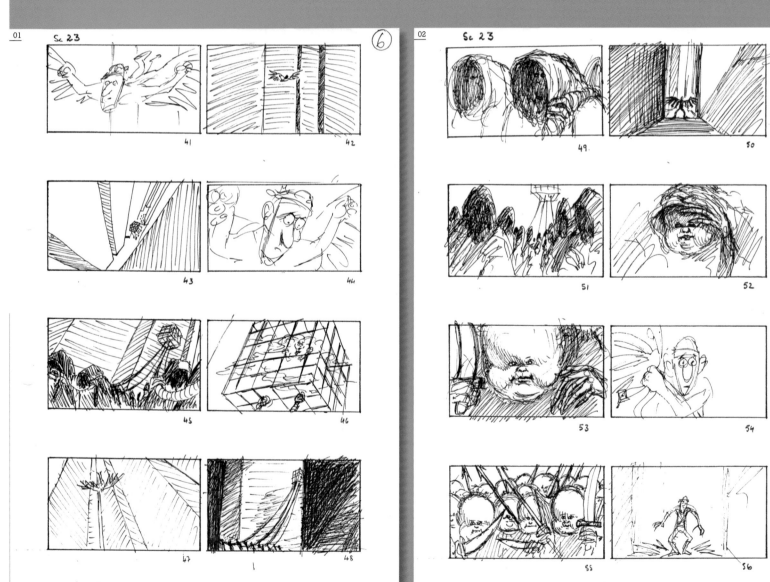

THE ADVENTURES OF BARON MUNCHAUSEN

(01–03) Gilliam may have a reputation for troubled productions, but he says he only went over budget on one film—the infamous **The Adventures of Baron Munchausen** in 1987, which he says, went "out of control before we even started shooting" and was "one of the many ends of my career. It was unproduced and Italianized," referring to the long and complex $46m production at Cinecittá Studios in Rome, which is fascinatingly documented in the book *Losing The Light: Terry Gilliam And The Munchausen Saga* by Andrew Yule. "The book is actually a soft version," he laughs. "You don't get half of what was really going on."

This, however, still remains one of Gilliam's finest and most ravishing films with a reputation now as a classic. "It's so strange that it worked out that way," he laughs. "Everything about it was a horror. I remember my assistant being unable to understand how we were producing this beautiful material by the end of each nightmare day. The images just floated and danced beautifully. I realize now when I look back that I was actually very strong physically and mentally. I don't know how I did it, but I could drive myself through anything. I don't have that drive now, that madness, that utter conviction." (02–03) Pages from Gilliam's original storyboards for the film.

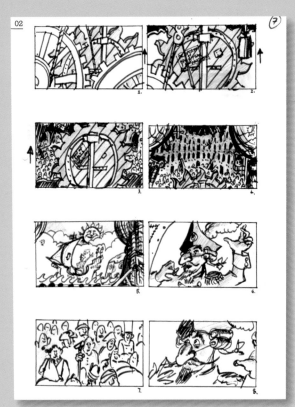

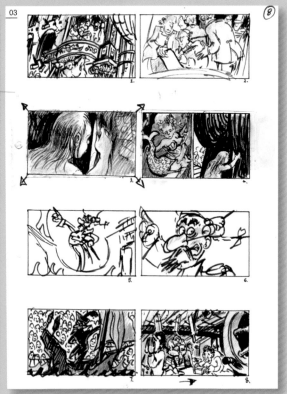

TWELVE MONKEYS

(**04**) Gilliam says that his stars—Bruce Willis and Brad Pitt—in **Twelve Monkeys** were cast against type. "I caught both of them at a time when they wanted to prove something," he says. "Bruce wanted to prove that he was a serious, interiorized actor and Brad was trying to show he was capable of being much more than a cool, pretty face. So they both worked incredibly hard at it." Pitt won an Oscar nomination for his supporting performance and was thought of in a new light after the film.

you choose well, spend time in advance making sure we are all talking about the same film, there is not much direction needed on the set. Usually if I've cast well, the actor understands what the character is very quickly.

I don't know how I achieve the visual side of things other than lots of work and attention to detail. I have a lot of energy and I know what I want. Oh yes, and I can draw. When we're writing, I make sure we're not writing anything that I can't figure out how to do. When the script is done, I start drawing the storyboard. I don't look at the script. I start drawing and things start changing. Another part of my brain goes into action and the act of drawing alters the way I see a scene, details change, new ideas merge, the scene begins to live. That's the motion-picture thing happening. I see a blank space and put something in it and, voilà, I've added a new problem or idea. Later we rewrite the script to incorporate these new thoughts.

For me, the most difficult and painful part of making a movie is the shooting. The writing and the planning are a joy because everything is potential; everything is going to be wonderful. The editing is exciting because it's a calm time,

trying to reassemble the jigsaw that fell apart during the shoot. The shoot is simply exhausting. You're always getting it wrong. At some point, the exhaustion is useful because I stop double thinking and worrying, and can just say, "OK, we've got to shoot." In the evenings, knowing I've made a mess of the day's work, I actually sleep well because I think, "Fuck this film! It's like warfare. It's like why the fuck did I get into this? Who was I kidding?" I just lie in bed thinking, "You fucking idiot, Gilliam. You jumped-up piece of shit." I then nod off.

I've had some problems with producers. But Chuck Roven on **Twelve Monkeys** was a very good producer. That was because he really knew his stuff. We fought much of the time, but he was smart. He got me to do things out of spite, but they worked out well, so it was an interesting balance. So many others I've worked with have either been too conciliatory or stupid, or not strong enough. Producing is a hard job because nobody's grateful to a producer, but I do respect good people. They tend to be the line producers because they are the pragmatic ones with practical filmmaking problems to solve, not the time-consuming political problems. →

I do feel a certain weariness now, I just turned 71. There was such blind enthusiasm when we were flying with **Monty Python**. **Brazil** was a nightmare and a studio battle, but it didn't matter because we won the battle. We kept going. **The Adventures of Munchausen** was utter madness and I remember at the end of it thinking that my ''career'' was over. That's why I broke all my rules, went to Hollywood, got an agent, put my head in the lion's mouth and made **The Fisher King**, **Twelve Monkeys** and **Fear and Loathing in Las Vegas**. Those were the easiest movies I've ever done.

Having said that, I don't like Hollywood, a small provincial village with a vast bureaucratic system. Its restricted mentality makes me crazy. It's an inverted pyramid: the talent supporting agents, managers, accountants, studio executives and so on and so on, wasting so much money in the effort. What irritates me most is the fact that the studios have so much more money to spend on marketing than the rest of the world. It's become almost impossible to compete with them. What Hollywood thinks is good is what we get to see. We are all poorer for that.

It's funny looking back on **The Adventures of Munchausen** now. David Puttnam greenlit it when he was running Columbia, but he was fired a couple of weeks before we started shooting, and Dawn Steel took over. Dawn said the studio would get behind the film if I cut it down to two hours; it was around two hours and five minutes. So I cut five minutes out and got it down to two. It opened with the best reviews the studio had had for years. But despite excellent business they released wide because, at the time, Sony was negotiating to buy the studio and the current owners decided the books would look much better by cutting releasing and marketing costs. So, along with several other films, they dumped **The Adventures of Munchausen**, only 117 prints in all, no marketing. And that box-office disaster made the story of the film perfect. Here is the smart-arse guy who beat the studios on **Brazil**. Now his new movie has gone way over budget and done no business. The guy has got his comeuppance. That's a great story! ❞

01 Gilliam on the set of **The Imaginarium of Doctor Parnassus**

02–06 The Imaginarium of Doctor Parnassus

07–08 Gilliam's storyboards for the film

Jean-Luc Godard

Jean-Luc Godard made a splashy entrance onto the international film world with his stunning debut feature **À Bout de Souffle** in 1960. The sixteen features and numerous shorts he made in the following decade represent perhaps the most exciting explosion of new cinematic thought and technique in the medium's history. Blending often radical politics, existentialist philosophy and a passionate cinephilia, Godard was the most influential of the Nouvelle Vague filmmakers who also included François Truffaut, Jacques Rivette, Eric Rohmer and Claude Chabrol, and the ultimate "auteur." Now 81, he still makes movies, although his experiments with form and narrative are increasingly obscure.

Godard was born in Paris in 1930 and developed his love of cinema while at university, spending day after day at the Cinémathèque where he met Truffaut, Rivette, André Bazin and the other cinephiles who would compose the

Nouvelle Vague movement ten years later. He, Rohmer and Rivette founded the film journal *La Gazette du Cinéma* and, when that proved short-lived, contributed extensively to *Cahiers du Cinéma*, rejecting classical French commercial cinema and espousing the merits of neglected US filmmakers like Nicholas Ray, Anthony Mann and Otto Preminger.

He made his first short **Opération Béton (Operation Concrete)**, about the construction of a dam in Switzerland, with his first 35mm camera in 1954, followed by **Une Femme Coquette**, an adaptation of a Guy de Maupassant story in 1955. After three more shorts, collaborations with his friends like Rohmer and Rivette, and continued writings for *Cahiers*, he made his first feature **À Bout de Souffle (Breathless)** in 1959.

Released in 1960, **À Bout de Souffle** proved a sensational success, opening in France in March that year and then receiving a festival launch at

01

01 Jean-Luc Godard with Anna Karina on the set of **Alphaville** in 1965

to the cinema of the past that he loved,
but they always felt startlingly original."

Berlin in June. Made on an ultra-low budget, featuring semi-improvised dialogue, dazzling handheld camerawork (Godard pushed cinematographer Raoul Coutard around in a wheelchair in many scenes), and a new style of jump cutting that dispensed with unnecessary scene-setting shots as well as creating an abrupt new rhythm, the film appeared spontaneous and fresh. It has influenced generations of filmmakers since.

After his first success, Godard was rapaciously prolific and unrelentingly controversial, both in subject matter and technique. His second feature **Le Petit Soldat** (1963) was banned in France for its subject of the Algerian War of Independence and **Les Carabiniers (The Soldiers)** (1963), about the futility of war, was received poorly in France, so much so that Godard wrote a defense of the film in the pages of *Cahiers*.

His films were filled with references to the cinema of the past that he loved, but they always felt startlingly original, from the masterful portrait of rotten cinema **Contempt** (1963) to the petty gangster drama **Bande à part** (1964) to the mesmerizing science fiction fantasy **Alphaville** (1965) and **Pierrot le Fou** (1965), a postmodern classic that merged reality and fantasy in its portrait of a man escaping his bourgeois lifestyle. The apotheosis of Godard's disillusionment with

contemporary society (and cinema) was **Week End** (1967), essentially the portrait of one long weekend traffic jam through which the troubles and violence of life are illustrated.

After **Week End**, which ironically concludes with the end-card "End Of Cinema," Godard became increasingly absorbed by political issues, developing an interest in Maoist ideology and making a handful of films and shorts with strong didactic messages. He had a renaissance of sorts in the 1980s with films like **Passion** (1982), **Sauve Qui Peut (La Vie)** (1979), **'Je Vous Salue, Marie'** (1985) and **Prénom Carmen** (1983), but his work has since become more self-mocking and inaccessible, as he apparently lost faith in the medium and industry of film. Godard's hostility to the cinema establishment is famous: he declined the offer to fly to Los Angeles to receive an honorary Oscar, nor did he attend Cannes for his last film **Film Socialisme** (2010).

"It's over," he told *The Guardian* in 2004. "There was a time maybe when cinema could have improved society, but that time was missed."

Perhaps his greatest achievement since **Week End** is his colossal **Histoire(s) du Cinéma**, made between 1988 and 1998. Told in eight parts, the film is a study of cinema in the context of the 20th century and as it relates to Godard's own life.

02 Pierrot le Fou

03 Bande à part

03

Amos Gitai

"I think I am a filmmaker of ideas. Probably one of the reasons
I became a filmmaker was to speak about things I'm interested in,
in a form I like. I think that's true of the filmmakers I like as well."

Israel's Amos Gitai is one of the world's most prolific filmmakers, with twenty narrative features and twenty-five feature documentaries under his belt since 1979, not to mention tens of shorts. His portraits of different facets of Israeli life in films like **Kadosh** (1999), **Kippur** (2000), and **Free Zone** (2005) have won him countless awards at the world's leading film festivals.

Born in Haifa, Gitai was studying architecture when the Yom Kippur war broke out in 1973, and he resolved to be a filmmaker after shooting Super 8mm footage of the fighting while flying helicopter missions in the war, missions that would be depicted in **Kippur** over twenty years later.

After a host of shorts, Gitai made his name making documentaries in the late 1970s, including **House** (1980), the story of a house in West Jerusalem, and **Field Diary** (1982), a diary shot in the occupied territories before and during the invasion of Lebanon.

After **Field Diary** received a controversial reception in Israel, Gitai moved to Paris in 1983, where he was based for ten years. There he began making fiction films such as **Berlin-Jerusalem** (1989) and a trilogy about the Jewish legend of the Golem. Returning to Haifa in the mid-nineties, he began a prolific output of films, most famously **Kadosh** set in Mea Shearim, the Jerusalem district of Orthodox Jews, and **Kippur**, a stunning memoir of his wartime experiences. Other films from this period include **Zihron Devarim** (1995), **Yom Yom** (1998), **Eden** (2001), **Kedma** (2002), and **Alila** (2003).

His film **Free Zone**, about a hazardous car journey from Israel into Jordan starring Natalie Portman, Hana Laszlo and Hiam Abbass, was his fourth in competition at Cannes and won the Best Actress award for Laszlo.

Several of his recent films are partly or entirely set in France and feature major French stars—such as **Disengagement** (2007) with Juliette Binoche and **Later (One Day You'll Understand)** (2008) with Jeanne Moreau—but all deal with the social and political situation of the Middle East and the Jewish condition.

Amos Gitai

"" The first time I held a camera was a Super 8 camera in the [Yom Kippur] war. Because the war started on 6th October 1973, and my birthday was just a few days afterwards, my mother bought me a little Super 8 camera a week earlier. So when I ran to the front, I took it with me and in the first days of the war, I filmed. I just filmed some faces, some textures of what we were flying over in the helicopter, and then I carried on after the war. I would make five-minute shorts on Super 8, and finally I got myself in front of the committee for the only Israeli TV channel that allowed me to do films up to 20 minutes long.

It was a very good period for TV, not just in Israel, but in many countries. You had extremely open-minded commissioning editors willing to experiment. My first film for TV was 18 minutes long and showed what I could see from the window of my apartment in Haifa. I cannot imagine that in today's world of ratings, I would ever be commissioned to do a film like that now.

It was a good apprenticeship because I believe you need to do some minor work in order to figure out what really interests you in cinema. Then I started to do my first documentaries for TV, and the one that was probably most well known was **House**, which I made thirty years ago.

House was the last of the documentaries I did for television and it doesn't have a voiceover. I chose one house west of Jerusalem in what is now called the German colony. I wanted to look at the biography of the house so it could be a metaphor for the Jewish experience. This particular house was owned by a Palestinian family, but that family left in 1948 and the Israeli government settled Jewish immigrants from Algeria in it. In 1967, the Algerian families were moved to housing in the territory of Jerusalem and it was taken over by a famous Israeli economist who converted it into a three-floor mansion. In order to do that, he brought in workers from the refugee camps on the west bank. So I decided to juxtapose fragments of the biographies of these workers into the human archaeology of Jerusalem.

01 Gitai with Natalie Portman and Hana Laszlo during the filming of **Free Zone**

It was one of the earliest films that questioned the identity of and rapport between Israelis and Palestinians, and I think the form of the film showed me that I wanted to use cinema to keep searching. By form, I mean that it was a blend of biographies next to each other, which themselves create the narrative structure and the meaning. You don't need to spoon feed the audience, because the structure itself allows the viewer to see the meaning. The house became a metaphor for the larger Jerusalem.

I don't give easy answers in my films. I like to collect human contradictions and avoid the schematic and simplistic. It's very problematic in the Middle East where the dialogue is so intoxicated that if you start to play the role of one against the other, it's the end of it. So you have to install the complexity that exists in reality as much as you can, and trust the viewer that they will keep going with the work that you have started. You give them material and they have to keep interpreting it.

Esther (1986) was my first fictional film and I chose the Old Testament book of Esther as my text. I was living in Paris at the time and decided to write to a great French director of photography, Henri Alekan, who did films like **La belle et la**

> "I don't give easy answers in my films. I like to collect human contradictions and avoid the schematic and simplistic."

bête (1946) for Cocteau and **La bataille du rail** (1947) for René Clément, and later on **Wings of Desire** (1987) for Wenders. I asked him to direct a series of tableaux about the narrative, which is about a cycle of repressions, about people who are persecuted and how they persecute themselves when they get power. And Alekan said yes, he would love to do it and he came with me to Israel.

That was fascinating. In a way, since I had never been to film school, I thought the best way I could learn was from the best, so I learned a lot from him. He told me a lot about the great work he had done; he came from a generation of cinematographers who had to challenge the negative when it was much less elastic and sensitive, so he would create layers of light. We did four films together.

Similarly, in **Golem, The Spirit of Exile** (1992), I asked a number of directors to act in the lead roles, including Samuel Fuller and Bernardo Bertolucci. I wanted to have people I respected on my set. I told them that I had a great relationship with my mother and she always told me to go after the best. I was just following the advice of my mother, that's all.

Fuller is very different from Bertolucci, of course, and Alekan is different from later cinematographers, but I wanted to be exposed to them, not just be viewing film or reading but having a direct dialogue. They were very generous. I remember Bertolucci even insisted that he would not be paid, not even for his flight from Rome; he was on a jury, which gave me a big prize for **Esther**, and he loved it.

On **Esther**, I was very shy to work with actors. I was really interested in situating the text in landscapes and seeing the relationship between sets and texts, and the narrative. Rightfully, my actors complained at the time that I was not really interested in them. Only since **Devarim**, where I actually acted myself, have I started to be more interested in and more sensitive to the actors.

Devarim was the first film I made after I had gone back to Israel in the early 1990s and it started a very productive period for me. I chose

a book by Ya'ackov Shabatai who was one of the few writers who looked at contemporary Israel and wrote the first screenplay myself, but then I asked playwright Gilad Evron to do a draft and then, like I do with most films, did a final version when I was close to shooting.

I focus more on structure than writing lots of different notes. In **Devarim**, which is an adaptation of an existing novel, the dialogue in the film was based on the dialogue in the book, and I was determined to think cinematographically on the structure. The book was written as a continuous, fragmented sentence, but I took the two lead characters, Caesar and Goldman, and shot Caesar's scenes in continuous, uninterrupted shots, because of all his male conquests and intimate relations. And Goldman, who I played, was shot in much more fragmented sequences like pieces of memories because he is haunted by the presence of Europe and World War II. Caesar creates his own space, invades other spaces. But Goldman is limited and crushed by the spaces. →

02 Free Zone

YOM YOM

(01–03) After **Devarim**, **Yom Yom** was an original script—"a more liberating process," says Gitai, than adapting a novel—and unlike **Devarim**, which was set in Tel Aviv, **Yom Yom** was set in Haifa. In the film Moshe Ivgy (**01, 03**) plays a man with both Jewish and Arab blood, while Juliano Mer-Khamis (**02**) plays his amoral childhood friend.

"The story was borrowed from the actor Juliano Mer-Khamis, who really is a son to a Jewish mother and an Arab father," explains Gitai.

[Sadly Mer-Khamis was gunned down in April 2011 in the Palestinian city of Jenin; he acted in several Gitai films including **Kippur** and **Kedma**.]

"Haifa is a very tolerant city between Jews and Arabs, unlike the rest of Israel," says Gitai. "The fact that Arabs and Jews live together is normal there, it's not a scene of conflict like Tel Aviv, where such a community would be a political gesture. **Yom Yom** was a homage to that métissage as the French would say."

I am always thinking of shooting when I am writing. During the writing period I like to visit locations that give me some elements that I integrate into the writing and casting.

I like to speak to my actors a lot before we shoot, to understand the universe they come from; they tell me their personal stories, what moves them and what is important to them. I would find it difficult to direct somebody that I am not interested in at all. Otherwise it would be strictly mechanical. I have to find something interesting in them and then I think I know how to direct them.

I don't like my actors to have marks. I know some DPs love it, but I prefer that they move naturally and compose the shot themselves. It's not a complete improvisation in the sense that we've had a long preparation period for the film and I like the actors to come in early and inhabit the sets before we shoot. The actors from **Kadosh** were coming to locations two or three months before shooting, for example.

I have been in situations where it came about later on that I didn't like the actor or found them too self-conscious or self-important. It's a different experience working with professionals and

LATER

(04–06) Gitai was first presented with the novel **Plus Tard (One Day You'll Understand)** by its author Jérôme Clément, who was also at the time the head of influential French broadcaster ARTE. "He told me that he was baptized after he was born, was a choir boy at the local church when he was a child, and in possession of all the proper certificates of French society, when one day he found out that his mother had told his son, not even him, that she was Jewish. When she died, he found a letter in his father's papers from 1941 telling the authorities that he was Roman Catholic and that his wife was Jewish. To write such a letter at that time meant that you were essentially giving up your wife to a terrible fate."

Clément asked Gitai to direct the story, which stars Jeanne Moreau (**06**, seen here with Gitai) as the mother and Hippolyte Girardot (**04**) as the son. "In **Later**, I decided to stick very closely to the characters and not make a big statement about France in the 1940s. What generalisms you learn, you learn from the handful of characters."

non-professionals. With non-actors or young actors, you have to solicit or encourage them to construct something, but with very established actors, you have to convince them to do something they have not done before, and sometimes they resort to tricks that work for them. To me as a viewer, I get very discouraged when I see an actor using techniques from which I can figure out immediately what they're trying to do. The work for me is to get them to invest in the project and dare to find capabilities they don't even know they have.

I look at every film like an open diary, each one as separate, and I include in each one

different things that make me think or touch me or move me or disturb me or make me furious, and at the same time I like to experiment with aesthetics and form because cinema is not just narrative to me. It's a craft that has a narrative component, but also visual and aural. It's a complete experience and each time I want to shape it in relation to what is the theme or narrative. Form is essential to me; it conforms to my background in architecture.

I think I am a filmmaker of ideas. Probably one of the reasons I became a filmmaker was to speak about things I'm interested in, in a form →

KIPPUR

(01–06) Gitai's most personal film—and perhaps his best—is **Kippur**, his account of his own experiences in the 1973 Yom Kippur war, including the moment when his rescue helicopter was shot from the sky, which almost killed him. The film is a wrenching, urgent account of the struggle and monotony of daily war.

"The person who encouraged me to do it was Samuel Fuller. On one of the evening breaks when we were shooting [**Golem, The Spirit Of Exile**], I told him my story of the war, and after that he never left me alone, saying that I had to make this film. It was very difficult to make because we made it 27 years after the incident. I wanted to instill the feeling of chaos, which is what war is. I watched a lot of war films before I did **Kippur** and the problem is that they describe war in much too orderly a manner. War, in my experience, was chaotic and doesn't work out according to plan. Essentially it's a rupture and that's why I framed the film with two scenes of

lovemaking. After **Kadosh**, I wanted to show the sensual ritual of love between a man and a woman, which is brutally broken by the war. It takes you from your routine and throws you into this hell and expects you to function in it. So in directing the war scenes in **Kippur**, it took a lot of thinking to keep the freshness, not to make them too rigid, but just to maintain the strength and intensity of the war experience."

The helicopter crash itself is a shocking moment, which captures the terrifyingly random nature of life and death in combat situations. "I think that crash is one of the reasons I did **Kippur**," says Gitai. "Obviously I will always remember this incident in which I almost died and in which the co-pilot was decapitated by the missile just a meter away. Luckily, the second pilot managed to fly three more minutes and get away from the Syrian fire, and crash on the side of the Israeli forces. The incident didn't take very long but it was a shattering thing to go

"I look at each film like an open diary, each one as separate, and I include in each one different things that make me think or touch me or move me or disturb me or make me furious, and at the same time I like to experiment with aesthetics and form because cinema is not just narrative to me. It's a craft that has a narrative component, but also visual and aural."

through. An incident like that can crush you, but I felt that in the very severe school of Israel, I had passed the ultimate exam, and had gained my right to express what was on my mind and in my heart."

The film is also impressive for the scale of the rescue sequences and the vivid recreation of combat. Gitai, flush from the international success of **Kadosh**, shot on 35mm with three Panavision cameras going at the same time to catch as much coverage as he could. The production rented tanks and helicopters from the Israeli army, the actors were put on a rigorous training schedule for three months before shooting and UK effects specialist Digby Milner of **James Bond**, **Star Wars** and **Harry Potter** fame was hired to engineer the real on-set explosions, including the helicopter crash.

"He said the easiest thing would be to shoot from the exterior while you explode the helicopter, but I said that I wanted to see the human faces in this moment. For me the human face is the mirror of the war. They are my point of view. This was complicated because there was one machine at Pinewood Studios in London that could enable this and so we shipped it over."

Similarly powerful is a scene in which the rescue soldiers are attempting to lift a casualty on a stretcher and carry him through a sea of mud (**05**). "It was a terrible day and the producer called from Tel Aviv to cancel the shooting because it was too foggy to land a helicopter where we were. He said we could do it on blue screen. But I didn't like this idea and went to my actors, who agreed to go ahead and do it anyway. The scene was ready and I asked one of my assistants to tape off an area of mud so that nobody walked on it and it would be untouched before we started shooting. It was icy cold and we did it. It was kind of a cinematic miracle."

I like. I think that's true of the filmmakers I like as well. I was thrilled to win the Roberto Rossellini Prize twice because I think he was very interested in the story of the place and the country he lived in, and that shaped very powerful and original cinema. We know so much about post-war Germany from Fassbinder, but in such very original, sometimes mellow, sometimes documentary cinema.

I would say there is this family of filmmakers across borders, and their work exposes something about the territories they live in. I wouldn't know much about Iran from newspapers or television, for example, if I hadn't seen the cinema from there. Film is the hidden story of these countries. It's about ideas, history, but it's also the current of cinema.

There is nothing better than cinema to speak about Israel. And sometimes there can be great surprises. After **Kippur** played in Cannes, I got a call from Youssef Chahine, who said that he thought it was the best film in Cannes. He got into trouble for saying that to the newspapers when he got back to Cairo. So sometimes a film can cross borders.

My work is very connected to a state of mind, and I'm not sure I would be able to shoot **Kippur** today in Israel because it humanizes the image of what it is to be a soldier and Israel is going in such a dangerous direction politically that it wouldn't be allowed.

The government has talked about passing a law where filmmakers will have to declare loyalty to the state. If we make strong cinema that is homage to the culture that produced it, and if that cinema includes views that are critical to the state, that too is homage to the culture that produced it. Why limit that? Why destroy it?

01 Gitai with Juliette Binoche
on the set of **Disengagement**

02 Juliette Binoche as Ana
in **Disengagement**

Titles

Gitai's films have always achieved wide festival and art house distribution exposure around the world, but he insists contractually that the films are exhibited with the Hebrew title intact. Hence **Kadosh** is known worldwide as Kadosh, and not as Sacred, which is the English translation. Likewise **Devarim**, **Kedma**, **Alili**, **Yom Yom** et al.

"I chose the titles intentionally," he explains, "to create the legitimacy of the language in the title of the film. The synonymy of the language is part of these films."

KADOSH

(03–04) One of Gitai's greatest achievements was his 1999 film **Kadosh**, a lyrical and harrowing story about two sisters in an ultra Orthodox Haredi community; one, Rivka, who is married, but cannot conceive and one, Malka, who is in love with someone else, but who is instructed to marry a man within the community.

"That film was a very fulfilling experience," says Gitai, who cast well-known model and TV celebrity Yaël Abecassis as Rivka **(04)**.

"People who worked with me in casting advised me against Yaël because she was too beautiful and too much of a star, but I cast her in the role so long as she took six weeks off her TV talk show to plunge into the universe of this very marginal community. Later she asked me why I chose her, and I told her I was trying to break the caricature of the religious as ugly. For me it was the most terrible thing that this beautiful and delicate character would be driven to her own death through the love of God, and the film would be more effective if she played the role."

For the film, Gitai adopted a more deliberate pacing than in his preceding work. "The ceremonial aspect of religion is about rhythm and, whether you are in a church or mosque or synagogue, we move objects in space in a certain rhythm. That is a part of the attraction of religion today, because it offers relief to the hustle and bustle of the contemporary world. I had a long discussion with my French producer who thought I should speed it up and I said, 'No, that is what the film is about. It's not just the text or the words, it's about rhythm and ceremony.' Every Saturday evening, when we were preparing the film, we went with the actors to see the speech of the Rabbi of Jerusalem in the synagogue."

Paul Greengrass

"The power of the collective is immense in films. When a film works, it is never because the director was good. It's because everyone was good. Always. There has never been a film in history where it was brilliantly directed, but not very well performed or written."

Although he has made relatively few theatrical features, Paul Greengrass has been involved in making film and television since he left Cambridge University and went to work at Granada Television. He became a producer/director on the highly regarded current affairs program **World in Action** where he worked for a decade, traveling around the world covering conflict and issues of public concern. He co-wrote the book *Spycatcher: The Candid Autobiography of a Senior Intelligence Officer* with former MI5 assistant-director Peter Wright, which the UK government attempted to ban for its insight into intelligence matters.

After *Spycatcher* he moved into TV drama, keeping his interest in real-life events by making films like **Resurrected** (1989), **The One That Got Away** (1996), **The Fix** (1997), and **The Murder of Stephen Lawrence** (1999).

His career would get an unexpected boost by **Bloody Sunday** (2002), another riveting documentary-style TV film about the Bloody Sunday massacre of 26 civilian protesters by British soldiers in Northern Ireland in 1972. Its exposure at the Sundance Film Festival that year—where it was acquired for theatrical release in the US—would lead to Greengrass being hired by Universal Pictures to direct **The Bourne Supremacy** (2004), a sequel to the 2002 blockbuster **The Bourne Identity** starring Matt Damon. Greengrass applied his visceral handheld style to the franchise, creating nerve-crunching action sequences that left many in the audience reeling.

It proved a winning combination and a box-office smash, leading to another Bourne movie, which was even more successful, **The Bourne Ultimatum**, in 2007. Meanwhile, in 2006 he used his new-found clout to make a documentary-style recreation of the hijacking of United Airlines' Flight 93 on September 11. The film, **United 93**, was highly acclaimed and won him a BAFTA and Oscar nomination for direction.

His most recent film, **Green Zone** (2010), was an adaptation of the book *Imperial Life in the Emerald City* by Rajiv Chandrasekaran detailing alleged mistakes made by the US military in Iraq. The film, budgeted at over $100m, again starred Matt Damon.

Paul Greengrass

"I started at **World in Action**, which was a phrase coined by John Grierson. It was a very important program on British television at that point and always had been. I'd grown up with it and loved its choice of subjects and anti-establishment, non-metropolitan sense of attack. I loved its filmmaking, which was very, very direct and, of course, classical in the British sense because it went back to Grierson.

The programmers were unmediated. It was straight documentary with narration and sometimes without, and it was a strange, eclectic mix of documentary filmmaking and investigative journalism, the very best traditions of popular journalism. It had an international agenda, a left-of-center, radical hue and was very rigorous in its filmmaking and approach to the factual world. It maintained eye level with its audience, unlike the BBC, which had always had a metropolitan stance, talking down to its audience.

So when you marry all those elements up, you can see that it was a very rigorous training for filmmaking of a certain type and expertise. It had a powerful effect on me and it prided itself on its clear, economical, driving storytelling.

I made lots of films of different kinds and in different conditions. Sometimes you would make them over a weekend, others would take over a year. I started as a researcher and after a few years became what they used to call producer/directors. You were given a tremendous amount of responsibility as a researcher. You teamed up with a producer and went out as a pair on the road.

I don't want to over-idealize it. Bad programs were made, but as a place that marked me, and still does, it's impossible for me to over-estimate. In fact, I once said, and I meant it, that I started on a program called **World in Action** and I've carried on making programs about the world in action. That's how I see it.

The first program I did was about the secret and grubby financial history of Manchester United Football Club. It got a lot of press at the time and was an awesome insight into the power of the program. The next program I did was in Northern Ireland, as the IRA Hunger Strikes started. I ended up shooting inside the Maze Prison—the first time that had happened at that point—interviewing the hunger strikers, and shooting inside the dirty cells with shit all over the walls. The experience of the Troubles, Northern Ireland, political violence and conflict had a profound impact on me as a young man. That was the first time I went to Derry [where Bloody Sunday took place]. And I really felt I had unfinished business there, which is one reason I later made **Bloody Sunday** there.

I spent a lot of time traveling and shooting abroad—in the Middle East, South America and the US—often dangerous places, war zones, places of conflict. I remember we all got arrested in South Africa filming undercover about conditions under apartheid. Looking back, the whole **World in Action** experience—meeting Provos in the middle of the night, or being in Beirut at the height of the Israeli attacks, or Buenos Aires when the Belgrano was sunk, or the Philippines during the revolution—it was all an education in life as well as filmmaking.

After about seven or eight years, I began to realize that I wanted something more. To make films with I suppose more ambition. I don't think I was quite aware that I had that feeling for a while or quite articulated it to myself. I think the

01   James Nesbitt in **Bloody Sunday**

01

> "Film directing is synthesis: The product of countless choices. Filmmaking is will plus technique plus vision. But your vision is the most important."

desire to write and direct films—movies—was a bit of a secret I dared not own up to, for quite a long time. **World in Action** was quite an insular world, and to express an aspiration to make movies would have been considered laughable, or a load of wank—or worse of all you were liable to be a sell-out, so it was a secret aspiration.

At the very end of my time [at **World in Action**], I had one great big adventure, which was the *Spycatcher* episode. I'd done quite a few programs about spies and spying. And the last one was about this renegade M15 officer who spilled the beans about the whole Philby, Burgess and MacLean scandal. Afterwards we decided to write a book together, and I took leave of absence to write it. When the British Government banned it, I had to take more time off to fight the court case and I think that was really when I decided my **World in Action** days were over.

While I was away in Australia, I wrote what would become my first film, **Resurrected**. Somewhere in the *Spycatcher* experience, I knew that I needed to move on. This was the biggest controversy I had ever been involved in and I just didn't want to be defined by that. I didn't want to become known as Paul "Spycatcher" Greengrass. I used to read that in the papers and feel utterly depressed. I was just 30 at the time. I wanted to see if I could make films, dramatic pieces, as opposed

to documentaries. Looking back, that was always my dream. I just needed to grow up a bit, mature and gain a bit of confidence to start to try.

My film education came at school initially, in two ways. I spent most of my time in the art room and they happened to have an old camera in there and a friend and I started making little films in there. That was absolutely critical for me when I was about 17. I had always been interested in taking photographs and one day—it was like a →

02–03 Scenes from **Bloody Sunday**

04 Paul Greengrass

"Setting a tempo as a filmmaker is absolutely fundamental: It comes from the very first moment— it defines the builds, and the peaks and troughs."

light going off in my head—the power of the moving image struck me, and the limitless possibilities. From then on, I wanted to work with moving images, first in television obviously where it was easier to get work. At the same time, there was a teacher at school who ran a film club and I would go every Monday night to see seminal films like **À bout de souffle**, **Z**, **The Battle of Algiers**, **The War Game**. Every one was a classic.

When I left **World in Action**, I had to learn to swim and learn fast. I needed to learn the craft and I soon realized there was much much more to making films than I imagined. At first it went okay, but then I realized I wasn't getting it right; I couldn't make films be like I imagined they would be. They always seemed to fall short. And I remember the period around the making of **The Theory of Flight** as being a moment in my life when I knew something was not right at all.

I remember one moment very distinctly. I made a film called **The One That Got Away** (1996) about the SAS operation behind the lines in Iraq. I had written the screenplay and felt good about it. I thought it said what I wanted to say about the war and it was an interesting story about a man who'd gone in as an SAS professional and got separated from his unit, and had an epiphany on the other side. It was about his lonely walk to becoming a different person.

I was shooting a night scene with eight soldiers on patrol on a flat desert landscape in South Africa, which might sound simple, but is a prodigious technical challenge. Dialogue scenes involving many voices are always a nightmare, but we also had a lot of eyelines that were constantly changing, so there were problems of rigidity and fluidity, and also issues of veracity because you need to have some light to see the soldiers, but they are undercover so they shouldn't really be visible.

And I remember—it was a vivid epiphany for me—feeling that I wasn't doing it well. I just remember staying on set and thinking this is just not fucking right. It was a frustration that I didn't possess enough skills yet to render my vision

of what I wanted the film to be. I could see it in my mind, but I couldn't execute it. I hadn't found my voice. I knew it was there, but couldn't somehow express it.

I've looked back at that moment many times, as the moment when all the frustrations of that period resolved themselves. Somewhere out of that frustration I resolved to commit to me, solely and I suppose uncompromisingly to what I wanted to say and how I wanted to say it. Which oddly was how I'd always been on **World in Action**. From then on, from **The Murder of Stephen Lawrence** onwards, I turned a corner. I think it was a combination of having seen things clearly failing, mixed with an evolving and strengthened sense of confidence in what it was I wanted to say. I had made quite a few films by then, so was getting better, but it was about finding voices and becoming more technically adept. It's like anything. The more you do it, the better you get.

By **The Murder of Stephen Lawrence**, I felt I had found out how to execute scenes with the choreography and confidence that you see in the later films. Then I went onto **Bloody Sunday** when I was trying to do the things I did in **The Murder of Stephen Lawrence**, but execute them more as a theatrical film. Looking back, I think I can draw a line from watching **The Battle of Algiers** as a teenager at school, to working on **World in Action** as a young man and engaging with the world and seeing it at first hand, to the films that I now started to make at that period.

In **Bloody Sunday**, there was a scene when the politician's at the hospital watching the unfolding aftermath of this terrible event. Well, I can remember vividly being in a hospital in Beirut. We went to a hospital to shoot during an Israeli air raid, and they brought in a young boy, about 12, who had his legs blown off, and it was just appalling. I can think of many similar sorts of experiences, and when you have seen those events for real, they mark you.

So when you come to mount similar events, like in **Bloody Sunday**, you have experiences and insights that you can bring to your film. It's not →

UNITED 93

(01–05) Greengrass says that **United 93** was "a very blessed film. It was an example of what happens when everybody from floor sweeper to studio head pulls together. A certain sort of film becomes possible."
(01) Greengrass on the plane set talking to the cast.

THE BOURNE ULTIMATUM

(01–04) "Unlike all those franchise heroes, Bourne really is a counter-culture hero. He's against them and he's for us. It's an us-and-them-type film. Whereas the characters in other big franchises are great in different ways, like **Batman**, they are really the supreme evocation of America's restless insecurities and over-confidence. **Bourne** was quite different in that the character and the world had its roots in American cinema of the 1970s. Films like **Three Days of the Condor** or **The Parallax View**. It took an important thread in American cinema and brought it up to date—showed that that way of looking at the world was relevant again in the early 2000s. The franchise had an edge and attack about it. The character was saying to the audience, they are up to something and we need to find out what it is, and they are going to kill us if we try. I thought I could pull that out much more explicitly and that it would resonate with what was happening in the world, and still keep it commercial. I also felt that by compressing the stories into a limited timeframe, I could make you feel like you were there, that you really believed it was happening. I could imbue it with a sense of veracity. You would be with Bourne on this ride." (01) Greengrass with Matt Damon on location at Waterloo Station in London.

THE BOURNE SUPREMACY

(05–06) Of the Bourne movies Greengrass says they were "hugely exciting films to make," while conceding that the studio was a tad nervous at the visceral, dizzying action sequences he delivered in **The Bourne Supremacy**, which literally puts the audience into the frame and left many feeling temporary motion sickness. "Once the studio realized that people could handle it and that is how they understand images today, they were 100 percent behind us."

Creating an iconography

"I felt that I could create a Bourne iconography, which I did by removing all the costumes. If you look at the first film, he changes costumes a lot. I wanted him just in the one. In **Bourne Supremacy**, he just has the little coat (05–06) and a jacket from the beginning to the end of **Bourne Ultimatum** (01–04)."

"As a director, you have to accept that you are jack-of-all-trades and master of none."

the same as saying it's reductive. It's not equal. It's the product of your life that you are bringing to your judgments in your mature films. Film directing is synthesis: The product of countless choices. Filmmaking is will plus technique plus vision. But your vision is the most important.

And you have a responsibility when you are recreating real events, like in **United 93**. I keep going back to it, but **World in Action** taught me the power of humility and that is important in filmmaking, which is a very egotistical business. Directors have big egos—you just have to have. You have to think you know the answers. But on the other hand, the best filmmaking is profoundly an exercise in humility. An understanding that you are there to serve the film, the story, the performances. That the film is best when you take yourself out of it, to be able to hear the still small voice of the film itself. **World in Action** taught me a certain sort of self-confidence, almost arrogance, to engage with the world. But it also inculcated you in the opposite direction— and a very good direction—which is to take yourself out of it. It was unmediated filmmaking. There were no reporters on screen telling you the story. The story spoke for itself.

I can see that one of the things I try to do in films is to get to it from underneath. That was very much the case in **United 93**: let's just remove ourselves and look at this as if we were there, and what that says to us. In that film, it was about creating a company. They were a superb group of actors and we were all trying to achieve a shared mission. The power of the collective is immense in films. When a film works, it is never because the director was good. It's because everyone was good. Always. There has never been a film in history where it was brilliantly directed, but not very well performed or written. It just never happens. As a director, you have to accept that you are jack-of-all-trades and master of none.

You have to select the right people, of course, and be clear about what it is you are trying to do. You have to empower them very heavily and be their closest collaborator, helping them sift

through what's right and what's wrong. You are their mirror and their closest guide.

The most exciting thing about making films is that when you work with people and they fit with you, it's a bit like being a band. If [editor and collaborator] Christopher Rouse calls me saying that he's seen the rushes and he thinks this or that, it determines what I need to shoot the following day. Or if you are talking to Matt Damon, or any other actor for that matter, and you're feeling your inner instincts reinforced and organically building from each other, you are seeing the same thing.

Making films is about seeing a mountain through a mist and you get a glimpse of it every now and then, but most of the time you're steering toward it by your collective inner compass. When it works making a film, it's thrilling. Hopefully I've got a long way to go, but when I'm very old and look back, the moments I'll remember are the moments when you watch brilliant actors being at work with brilliant people, and bottling that energy, capturing it like the dreamcatcher. You look at Barry Ackroyd or other talented people and just see this indefinable other dimension being created for a moment and then being captured.

I was reading in the paper the other day about the Higgs boson particle and this guy was saying they've seen a little indication of it and they are trying to capture it. And I thought, that's what I do as a film director. I am trying to find these little bits of the fourth dimension and capture them. Because that's what film is: You are watching something that isn't real, yet it plays to your conscious and unconscious mind. For the moment you watch—it is real.

You know when you've got a piece of it. You don't know if you've got the whole thing right until incredibly late in the day—that is in flux right until the thing is finished. But you know when you have got a piece. You are looking to harvest the magic all the time. ”

Action and tempo

Some of the action sequences in the Bourne films—like the Moscow car chase in **The Bourne Supremacy** or the Morocco foot chase in **The Bourne Ultimatum** are among the most thrilling in movie history (**01**). Likewise, the epic night chase sequence in Baghdad in **Green Zone** (**02–03**). Greengrass says that realizing these scenes is "all about detail."

"It's about judging and selecting the detail and orientation that you need and marrying that with pace and attack," he says. "In other words, if you push hard and there's no detail and no orientation, you just get a mush. It's to do with how you shoot, how you cut and how you mix, and I have a great relationship with Christopher Rouse, who is one of the greatest editors in the world. Truly one of the all-time greats."

He says that the action scenes don't work by shooting a lot of coverage, which can then be cut down later.

"It's not coverage that I want," he explains. "It's more about trying to get it how I want it with the right kind of detail at the right rhythm. Tempo is very important in directing, as much as it is in conducting too. Setting a tempo as a filmmaker is absolutely fundamental: It comes from the very first moment—it defines the builds, and the peaks and troughs. It determines how quick you want to play a scene and conversely where you want to slow it down. Tempo gives you the ability to control variety. Control of tempo is what controls shape. Naturally," adds Greengrass, "that tempo needs to change multiple times during one film. It's got to change, it's musical. It's almost a thing you can convey to actors non-verbally. It's a performance art."

Michael Haneke

"I usually shoot about three minutes a day. I am a little hothead and won't stop until I have what I want. It takes time to redo it until it's right."

Although born in Germany, Michael Haneke was raised in Austria and after early roles as film critic and TV editor, he settled as a director, working in television from 1974. He achieved great success in TV, with films such as **Lemmings** (1979), and **Who Was Edgar Allen?** (1985), that led to his first feature, **The Seventh Continent** in 1989. **The Seventh Continent**, along with **Benny's Video** (1992) and **71 Fragments of a Chronology of Chance** (1994), formed what Haneke called the "Glaciation" trilogy, and represented the "emotional glaciation" of Austria. They introduced themes that would resonate through his work of the assault of media, alienation from family and society, and random violence, and were told in stark, unemotional images, which left the audience to use its own imagination.

In 1997, Haneke scored an international cult hit with his startling and shocking **Funny Games**, which caused a sensation when it screened in competition at Cannes. In 2000, he made his first film in Paris—**Code Unknown: Incomplete Tales of Several Journeys** starring Juliette Binoche—and used French actors including Isabelle Huppert, Benoît Magimel and Annie Girardot in a Vienna setting for his 2001 film **The Piano Teacher**, another Cannes sensation from the novel by Elfriede Jelinek.

Hidden (Caché) in 2005 returned Haneke to Paris with Binoche again, and Daniel Auteuil, and won him his widest international success to date. After a muted reception for his shot-by-shot US remake of **Funny Games** in 2007, he roared back to acclaim with his stunning 2009 period piece **The White Ribbon**, an epic story set in a German rural community before World War I, which won him the Palme d'Or at Cannes, the Golden Globe for best foreign language feature and an Oscar nomination.

His latest film, **Amour** (2012), is another French-language film starring Jean-Louis Trintignant and Isabelle Huppert.

Michael Haneke

" I did TV films at first because I didn't have the financing or connections that were necessary to get into features, but they were good for me because I hadn't yet found my own language.

But then it became more difficult to make serious work on television, especially **The Seventh Continent**. A TV station in Germany wanted to work with me and asked me what I wanted to do. I told them I had this idea for this story based on a magazine article and it was dark and difficult. So they told me to write it and I did, and I really had the impression that this was the first time I found my real independent way of telling this kind of story. But when they read it, they turned it down. They said "No way."

So it was a good opportunity to move away from TV and try to get money for this as a film. It wasn't difficult to get the money for the film because I was quite well known from my TV work. But it was a turning point for me because I started writing this story in a completely different way to how I would have for TV. The first idea was to start by showing the end of the family and explain in flashbacks how they had got to this. But I didn't want to explain why this had happened,

and it was impossible to have flashbacks without explanation. So one day I realized that it would only work without the flashbacks. That was why TV didn't want to finance it, because they want explanations for everything. They don't like things that ask questions.

It's the matter-of-fact, everyday life that I wanted to show and I had to find an aesthetic to show it. So the aesthetic in **The Seventh Continent** was different to the TV films because of all the close-ups, although the work with actors and cameras was no different. The main difference was in the screenplay because you can be more complex in cinema than in television.

I stick very closely to my screenplay when I'm shooting. I am not very good at drawing, but now I make storyboards that are very detailed with a computer program and show camera angles and how each scene will play out. I always keep the book of storyboards with me and the whole team has a copy to know what is going on. If they have a question, they know they can ask me. Sometimes they say they understand what I mean when they have read the book and then on set, they have forgotten. You have to explain

CODE UNKNOWN

(01–05) The celebrated opening sequence of **Code Unknown** is an eight-minute tracking shot containing multiple characters and multiple situations in a busy Paris street. Haneke had worked out the scene precisely beforehand and took three days to complete it: one day rehearsal with actors and camera, one day rehearsal with actors, extras and camera, and the third day shooting. Bearing in mind that Haneke shoots about three minutes a day, it timed out roughly according to his usual output.

(01–02) The script showing two consecutive pages of the opening scene, both with indication to the long shot/lateral camera movement. The dialogue is on the same sheet in this case so that Haneke would have the German version included on the opposite side of the French translation.

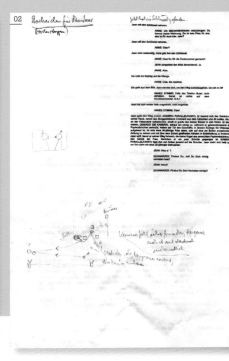

> "Very often the first take is the best because an actor is looking for their feelings, so they are really spontaneous. If you do it too often, they get tired and it takes a long time before they can be spontaneous again."

everything every day, but that's easy as I know exactly what I want.

Writing the script can be a complex process, although there are different ways I do it. First, I collect material based on a vague idea. If I am focused on this idea, many more things become apparent to me. Like if you are a pregnant woman, you are much more attuned to other pregnant women around you. That's normal. This collecting process can take months, sometimes years, because it depends how much you know at that time. If you just have a vague idea of the theme you are going to make a film about, it can take more time.

Once I have collected enough material, I make little cards, hundreds of cards, and I start to build the structure of the script and create scenes. I usually have three times as many cards as I ever use, of course. Then I put them on the wall. I have a vague idea of the beginning, the end, and the main points along the way. I work out how every character will develop with the cards and how to mix them up. And when all this is done, I start to write, which usually doesn't take long. At best, I can write the script in six weeks and it's really hard work. If you have a talent for dialogue,

writing is easy. It comes by itself. And if you have an idea for a certain character, it's easy to find the words.

I suppose the simplest example of how it works was **Code Unknown**. Juliette Binoche called me up, said she had seen my Austrian films and suggested we do a film together. I said I had to think about it. I had an idea to do a film based on the German word "fremde," which means "stranger" or "alien," and the first idea was immigration. I had considered doing this in Austria, but because of Juliette's call, I thought I could move it to France. Because I was not trained to do a French film, I went there for three months on a research trip and I met a lot of immigrants and slowly this story came to me.

Juliette Binoche is no stranger in Paris, she is a star, and because I wanted to make a realistic film, I thought a star can't play a normal person, so I decided to create a character who was an actress. So all these things came together. Of course, the main theme, and it's the main theme of all my films, is about communication.

I am very precise. The opening scene in **Code Unknown**, for example, which is a long tracking shot with multiple characters, was always →

CACHÉ

(01–02) Haneke was surprised that **Caché** was such a success with audiences, creating a frenzy both online and in intellectual circles. "I was surprised that England and America liked it so much because when I wrote the script, I thought it would be a film for certain intellectual film freaks. It's in the tradition of **Funny Games**, an auto-reflective film about cinema and media, although of course it has stars in Juliette Binoche and Daniel Auteuil **(02)** who brought in a bigger audience."

going to be done in one take. It was very difficult to achieve, and it would be impossible to do this if I had not written it. I had to find an idea of how the camera would move following one person and then another. You have to know it in the writing. I had worked out the exact movement and the exact location long before we shot it.

Of course, when I see something interesting while we are shooting, I try to incorporate it. On **Code Unknown**, in the final scene when the war reporter comes back to the apartment and can't get in, it started to rain. It was a surprise rain shower and came and went very quickly. The sky was getting darker and darker so we knew it might rain and we waited and then it came so we shot the scene. This was great, but in general I don't like surprises on set. Actors can give you pleasant surprises, something that is more than you sought out before, but that is not the normal way with me.

I don't work with actors before the shooting starts. If an actor is not stupid and is able to read a script, he will not do anything so far from what you have written. So if your depictions of human behavior are not stupid, he will do it. It's your profession as a director to know what is good for an actor. There is no way to teach how to direct an actor because every actor is different. It's the work the actor has to do, not the director. That's a question of feeling. You have to know how to treat every person, because every person is different and they need to be pushed a little. They need a forceful hand.

I think the acting in my films is pretty good. It's because I like actors, I come from a family of actors and my parents were actors. Shooting a film is a terrible experience and the only good thing is the work with actors, because the rest is all stress. You have thirty or forty people all working and thinking with their own heads and, while they will all do their best, they cannot be in my head knowing exactly what I want. So you have to deal with this contradiction and there is always stress in the effort to avoid things I don't like.

Of course, casting is half the work. If you have a good script and good casting, you have to be a big idiot to make a bad film. Bad casting can ruin everything, even if the actor is excellent. That is why I often write parts for certain actors because it makes things easier, even in the small parts. I know all the dangers. I also write a script for me as a director and similarly I avoid writing scenes that I am not sure I can do. It's the same thing.

I have had to change some actors, not very often, during production—once it was a leading part—and I always say it was my fault because it was a mistake in casting.

I don't do any rehearsal. The actors come on set, then I always do one take for technical purposes; they do the scene without emotion just to be clear for the camera. And then I start to shoot immediately. Very often the first take is the best because an actor is looking for their feelings, so they are really spontaneous. If you

do it too often, they get tired and it takes a long time before they can be spontaneous again.

So I will use the first or second take, or the twenty-fifth, but in between it is bullshit because people get exhausted. If you are doing very long shots, it can be difficult because one person can make a little mistake or the camera can pick up a little late. For example, in some of the big boulevard scenes in **Code Unknown**, we had one-day rehearsal with actors and camera for the ten-minute take. The second day, we rehearsed with actors, extras, and camera; the third day was shooting. And we had five minutes down fantastically when one extra looked into the camera and we had to start again. That's unusual of course.

I usually shoot about three minutes a day. I am a little hotheaded and won't stop until I have what I want. It takes time to redo it until it's right.

I don't show physical violence in my films for two reasons. First, because I think showing physical violence is a kind of obscenity I don't like. But second, I also think it's a positive thing to avoid this, because it's well known that if a viewer hears something dangerous and frightening, it's much stronger than if the doors open and there is a monster in front of you. I think you have to have a talent for creating tension and fear in your audience. The stories I tell aren't very funny and I think they affect people because they reflect people's own fears. I won't compare myself to Hitchcock, but he knew exactly where your fear was and exploited it.

There are, of course, essential scenes in each script. During the shooting you know where the essential scenes are and they have to be good. In **Funny Games**, it was the long scene after the death of the child. It is the film's most difficult scene and if it wasn't touching, the whole film would be much less gripping.

I am always thinking about the audience in my films, and how they will react. You have to think about them if you write a screenplay. If you write a novel, a reader can put it away and pick it up again later. But in the theater or cinema, if you lose the viewer, it's over. You have to always think what you can do that will keep them with you. To know this is the profession, and if you don't know this, you are not really a professional.

Of course, you can say things that people don't like to hear, but you have to say it in a way that they cannot resist listening to. It's not a question of what you are saying, but how you are saying it. Because film is manipulation. Always. So even if you have to make it clear to a viewer that he is being manipulated, you are manipulating him.

It's like in **Funny Games**. The moment one of the killers looks into the camera and tells you what you are thinking, I am showing the viewer that the film is artifice. And there are several points in the film where I pull you out of the illusion, just to show you that I can push you back in whenever I want. If I did it just once, you could maybe understand intellectually, but not emotionally. But I did it several times, and that →

FUNNY GAMES

(01–02, 06) Haneke describes the American version of the original **Funny Games**, his shot-by-shot English-language remake of **Funny Games**, as a "terrible" experience. "Firstly, I wasn't very confident with my English," he explains, "but also I underestimated how difficult it would be to find locations in the US that would allow me the same camera movement. The house we created in a studio, so that was the same as the Austrian version, but the exteriors were very, very difficult."

So why did he do it? "It was originally intended to be set in the US. The idea was that it was very American and the house in the first film is an American house—that kind of house doesn't exist in Austria. I saw the remake as like a Trojan horse, so we would do a certain kind of cinema with American stars in the US itself. That was the idea, but it doesn't work and I don't know why. The film is not bad, but it didn't find an audience." (01) Haneke's notes on the script with the storyboard and, importantly, a screenshot from the original version of the film so as to follow it shot by shot for the US remake. (02) Haneke on the set of the remake. (06) Naomi Watts, Michael Pitt and Brady Corbet in the remake. (03–05) The original 1997 version of **Funny Games**.

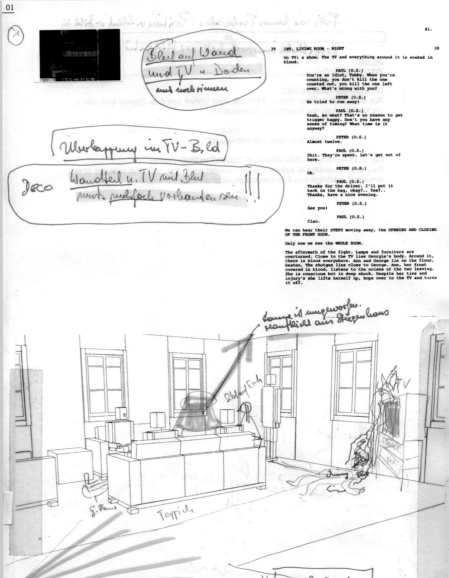

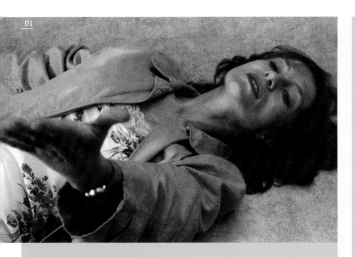

THE PIANO TEACHER

(01) This is the only film Haneke made based on pre-existing material. "Of all the cinema films I have made, this is the only one where not everything was from me," he explains. "I changed a lot from the structure of the novel. The first half of the novel follows the character when she was a teenager, so I was forced to invent another mother and daughter that don't exist in the novel to act as a mirror. A filmmaker friend of mine had asked me to write the screenplay for him, but he didn't get the finance to make the film, so it fell apart. Eventually the producer came to me and suggested that I do it. I said I had no real desire to make it, but would do so on the one condition that Isabelle Huppert play the part."

was the idea. I think you can't help but be reflective on the medium of cinema, especially after the experience we had from fascism and political manipulation through media. You cannot feed the illusion that film is reality. Look at German literature after the war, which was completely self-reflective, because we had seen what could happen when the platform was used with the wrong reality. I think it's the same in cinema. You have to reflect on your own medium and rules in the work itself. "

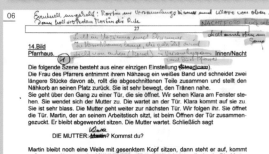

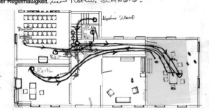

THE WHITE RIBBON

(02–07) Haneke originally wrote **The White Ribbon** as
a three-part mini-series for television in the late 1990s,
but various executive changes at the network meant that
it never happened. A decade later, Haneke's producer
Margaret Ménégoz read it and suggested that it be made
as a film "but that I had to cut out one hour." Haneke
worked with celebrated French screenwriter Jean-Claude
Carrière to hone down the TV script to a feature script.

"Obviously it was different because it was a period
film and I had to read a lot of books about education and
the country life of the early 20th century," says Haneke.
"We had researchers working on it and I think that
everything you see in the film is believable. I have spoken
to experts on the period who say that it is correct."
Haneke even brought in Romanian farmers to appear
as extras in the film. "Of the 200 extras, 100 came
from Romania to get those real weather-beaten faces,
because the German farmers today look different. They
do everything from air-conditioned tractors." (05–06)
Pages showing Haneke's storyboard and indepth notes
for the film.

Alfred Hitchcock

For a large part of his lifetime, Alfred Hitchcock was, if not dismissed, at least marginalized as a mere entertainer or "Master of Suspense." Highbrow critics acknowledged his technical skills, but felt frustrated that he appeared to limit himself to thrillers and melodrama, and failed to observe social issues or issues of importance. That perception changed in part as a result of the reverence accorded him by the French critics of the *Cahiers du Cinéma* in the 1950s, Truffaut, Godard, Chabrol, and Rohmer among them. Truffaut himself published a series of interviews with Hitchcock in 1967, and Chabrol and Rohmer collaborated on a 1979 book about the master, *Hitchcock: The First Forty–Four Films*. In the introduction to this volume, Truffaut recounts his confrontation by an American critic who was baffled at his praise for **Rear Window**. "You love **Rear Window** because, as a stranger to New York, you know nothing about Greenwich Village," said the critic. "**Rear Window** is not about Greenwich Village," replied Truffaut. "It is a film about cinema, and I do know cinema."

Hitchcock is now, of course, recognized by the world as one of 20th-century cinema's geniuses with a natural and fluid mastery of the medium that is technically, narratively, and stylistically unmatched to this date. His body of work between 1922 and 1976 is simply astounding, encompassing a range of masterpieces such as **The Lady Vanishes** (1938), **Rebecca** (1940), **Strangers on a Train** (1951), **Rear Window** (1954), **Vertigo** (1958), **North by Northwest** (1959), and **Psycho** (1960).

Hitchcock was born in London in 1899 and entered the film industry in 1920 as a title designer at Islington Studios in North London. He was retained as an assistant director and eventually promoted in 1925 to director on a film called **The Pleasure Garden**; however, it was his

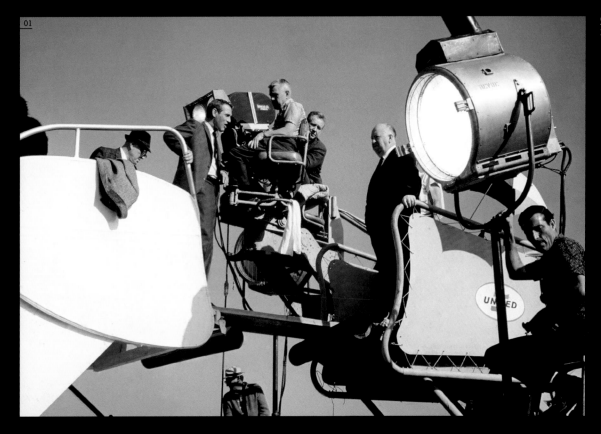

01

01 Alfred Hitchcock with Paul Newman in 1966

'Hitchcock is recognized by the world as one of 20th-century cinema's geniuses."

...hird film **The Lodger: A Story of the London Fog** (1927) that introduced his characteristic style and themes, which would later become legendary. The film is about a landlady who suspects her lodger is a serial killer and it is full of bold camera angles, menacing lighting, and special effects. **Blackmail** in 1929 was the first British film with sound, but it also featured Hitchcock's first chase sequence through a famous landmark, here the British Museum. These chases would become a trademark of his films.

In the 1930s, Hitchcock emerged as a star director in the UK with thrillers such as **The Man Who Knew Too Much** (1934), **The 39 Steps** (1935), **Secret Agent** (1936), **Sabotage** (1936), **Young and Innocent** (1937), and the near-perfect comedy thriller **The Lady Vanishes**.

Producer David O. Selznick poached him to come to the US and his first Hollywood film was an adaptation of Daphne Du Maurier's **Rebecca**, starring Joan Fontaine and Laurence Olivier. This won the Academy Award for best picture and Hitchcock a directing nomination.

Hitchcock clearly enjoyed exploiting the facilities and finances with which Hollywood furnished him, turning out a string of expertly executed thrillers, including **Foreign Correspondent** (1940), **Suspicion** (1941), **Saboteur** (1942), **Shadow of a Doubt** (1943), **Lifeboat** (1944), set entirely on a lifeboat, **Spellbound** (1945), with its famous Salvador Dalí dream sequence, and the celebrated romantic thriller **Notorious** (1946).

Perhaps his golden age was the 1950s, which kicked off with the superb adaptation of Patricia Highsmith's **Strangers On A Train** (1951) and included box-office hits like **Dial M For Murder** (1954) and **To Catch a Thief** (1955), a remake of **The Man Who Knew Too Much** (1956), tightly plotted nail biter **Rear Window** (1954), the note-perfect chase adventure **North by Northwest** (1959), and most memorable of all, his chronicle of obsession **Vertigo** (1958), which is considered by many one of the greatest films of all time, although it was not widely admired on its initial release.

Psycho (1960), probably Hitchcock's last great film, became the horror film by which all others would be measured. He made several more intriguing films including **The Birds** (1963), **Marnie** (1964), **Torn Curtain** (1966), and **Frenzy** (1972) before he died in 1980.

Known to have used storyboards extensively in preparation for his films, Hitchcock had a checkered relationship with actors, whom he believed should be entirely at the service of the director and the requirements of the film. That said, he elicited magnificent performances from the actors with whom he worked frequently like James Stewart, Cary Grant, Joan Fontaine, and Ingrid Bergman.

02 North by Northwest

03 Vertigo

Park Chan-wook

"I shoot and edit almost exactly to the storyboard.
There are minor changes depending on the production,
but I have spent a lot of time imagining every shot in
advance so there is really not that much to change."

Born in 1963, Park Chan-wook is a filmmaker from South Korea whose stylish, often violent films, such as his award-winning "Vengeance" trilogy, have set him apart as a world-class talent with a huge global fan base.

He was born and grew up in Seoul, and started his career working in various art departments, but quickly resolved to be a filmmaker. His first films—**The Moon Is the Sun's Dream** (1992), and **Saminjo (Trio**, 1997)—were not well received, so he started writing about cinema for Korean publications to make a living. However, his third film, **JSA: Joint Security Area** (2000), the story of a friendship that develops between guards on both sides of the North/South Korean border, was a spectacular box-office hit and became the biggest blockbuster in Korean history. Its fractured back-and-forth narrative and distinctive action sequences would signal what was to come from Park.

Sympathy for Mr. Vengeance (2002)—the first film in his trilogy about the futility of and devastation wrought by revenge—introduced Park to an even wider global critical fraternity, but it was his 2003 masterpiece, **Oldboy**, which established him as a visionary with absolute command of his craft. A visceral, shocking, elegantly crafted story of a man who finds himself kidnapped and imprisoned in a room for fifteen years, **Oldboy** won the Grand Jury Prize at the Cannes Film Festival and is being remade in the US with Spike Lee directing.

Lady Vengeance (2005), another grand and masterfully wrought story in which a woman brought together the victims of one evil man to wreak a collective vengeance on him, was a fitting end to the trilogy.

Park's romantic comedy and first HD film, **I'm A Cyborg, But That's OK** (2006), was less well received, perhaps because it was an unusual genre for him, but he was back on form with his visually stunning vampire saga **Thirst** (2009), which won the Jury Prize at Cannes.

In 2011, he unveiled his first film shot entirely on iPhone, **Night Fishing**, which he co-directed with his brother, Park Chan-kyong, and began production on his first English-language feature, **Stoker** (2012), starring Mia Wasikowska, Matthew Goode, and Nicole Kidman.

Park Chan-wook

"During my adolescence, my favorite films were James Bond movies. Even now in my writing process I have the habit of starting the film with a prologue before entering the narrative proper and I think that is a subconscious influence of the Bond films.

I never really watched much in my teens because the university entrance exams in Korea can be quite severe and they don't allow you time to do much else. But I did make a point of watching classics on TV with my parents at home every weekend. This was an invaluable experience for me, even though I watched everything in black and white, and I continually revisit these classics today because my only memory of them is in black and white.

Alfred Hitchcock, of course, is the director I admired the most from the early days when I decided to become a filmmaker, as well as Robert Aldrich. A few years down the track, I came to admire Ingmar Bergman and Michelangelo Antonioni, Douglas Sirk, Luchino Visconti and Akira Kurosawa. I count them as my major influences.

And last but not least, there are two Korean directors who inspired and encouraged me to become a director: Kim Ki-young and Lee Doo-yong. I say encouraged, not because I knew them personally, but because I was able to find the courage to step into filmmaking after seeing their films. In the early 1980s when I was a university student, Korean films tended not to

01 JSA: Joint Security Area

01

> **"Kim Ki-young, especially, is an influence to this day and I believe his filmmaking has seeped deeply into my modus operandi."**

be to my taste, but seeing the work of these two filmmakers I realized that these strange, crazy films could actually be made in Korea. Kim Ki-young, especially, is an influence to this day and I believe his filmmaking has seeped deeply into my modus operandi.

When I started out, there was a strong tradition of apprenticeship in the industry so you had to become an assistant to a director at the very lowest rung of the ladder. I worked as an assistant director on two features and was first AD on one of them. After that, and before I directed my first feature, I took on all sorts of things, basically in order to put bread on the table while ensuring I still had a foot in the door of the film industry. I wrote scripts, designed posters, prepared PR materials and even translated subtitles for English-language films. I got paid by film companies for these activities and finally was able to raise funding for a feature.

Around the time my first feature went into production in 1991, Hong Kong action films were in great demand and the request for my first film was to make something in that vein that combined romance, violence, and gangster elements on a shoestring budget. I put most of the blame for the film's failure at the box office on myself, although I had one excuse in that the leading man wasn't the actor I wanted at all, he was actually a singer and while he was a great singer, he was not really an actor.

I don't often get nervous. When I found myself on the film set for the first time, I felt that I had found my place. Given that the budget was tiny and the cast was not what I wanted, the only way to make the experience worthwhile was to establish a style for myself, and this was a way of making it cinematic. I experimented with elaborate transitions and played around with optical effects and camera movements to find the style. As someone who is so influenced by Hitchcock, especially **Vertigo** (1958), I thought I should do an homage to him in my first film and I used a dolly zoom, or the trombone effect as it's known. I am often labeled as a stylistic director and that is probably rooted in this first

experience: Rather than a creative experience at the time, it was more of a struggle, an effort to make something of this film.

Actually, on my second film, I took the opposite route and dialed it down, but I found that was not me. It was filled with cuss words and sex, and that would have been fine if I had done it in a B-movie manner like **Gun Crazy** (1950), but I was too concerned at the box-office failure of the first film so made a failed compromise. What I learned from that experience, and I tell young filmmakers in Korea this all the time, is not to be so concerned with failure or success at the box office, but know what you want, maintain it and indeed push it to the extreme limits.

By the third film, **JSA**, I had no intentions of making any compromises for the sake of commercial viability. I genuinely loved making that film, was very sincere on it, and made no compromises, and ironically it is the biggest grossing film of my career. I also learned to work with actors on **JSA**. Until then, I think I had become too preoccupied with the Hitchcock myth that he treated his actors like props and didn't treat his actors as artistic, creative collaborators. But doing **JSA**, we did a lot of rehearsals. I learned how to talk to the actors, listen to their often brilliant thoughts, and incorporate their ideas.

When I am writing, I don't like to write by myself. I like to have somebody sitting next to me with another monitor and keyboard and mouse connected to the same computer, so we are looking at exactly the same thing. To me it's like a piano duet. Somebody is writing away with one keyboard and the other person would add a response to that idea. That way we can share ideas on the same document and talk to each other. I just cannot stand the artistic solitude of writing alone and the shared process gets my gears into motion.

I write the final draft by myself and most of the critical elements of the film usually come about at this last stage. I don't feel any sense of solitude then because the basic structure is in place and I have a clear idea of where I need to go. At this →

OLDBOY

(01–03 and pages 150–151) This film was not an original concept, instead based on a celebrated Japanese manga, and Park says that it wasn't the vengeance theme so much as the idea of private incarceration that attracted him.

"I wanted to take the story from the manga to a whole new level," he explains. "The original deals with the question of why somebody would put the main character in a private jail for so long, but the answer was too flat, too bland, so I wanted to find a more apt motive. I realized that no matter what answer I could come up with wouldn't be a fresh or interesting idea, so I decided to change the question. The question shouldn't be, 'Why have I been imprisoned in a private cell for fifteen years?' It should rather be, 'Why have you let me go from the private cell? Why not leave me in the cell until I die?' That gave me the twist I was searching for and led to the outcome that you know from the film. With a mystery-thriller, people always tend to look for answers, but what I liked about this change to the original material was that it turns the idea on its head when I say shouldn't we ask the right question instead?" In the film's astonishing final shot, Park suggests that the lead character will remain in an incestuous relationship with his own daughter.

"The decision our protagonist makes is unthinkable for our society," he says, "but in a way, he is taking a heroic decision that he will not be tied down by the conventions that traditional society expects of him."

"Collaborating with the actors is the biggest joy I get out of filmmaking because everything else is planned during pre-production."

Creating an iconic sequence

One of Park's most iconic sequences is the beloved corridor fight sequence in **Oldboy** when the lead character returns to the location of his prison and fights his way out again (**03** and pages 150–151). Shot from the side as a stylistic tableau of action, it is considered one of the great hand-to-hand combat sequences in modern cinema and, ironically, was not storyboarded or planned in advance by the meticulous Park.

"I had storyboarded it in a completely different way," he says (see page 151). "Originally it was to be comprised of many hundreds of shots and I had in mind a multitude of unique shots, angles, movements, visual effects and moments to violence. I was determined to show everyone the ultimate fighting sequence. I wanted to shoot it as a master shot from beginning to end, and even if there were mistakes along the way, it wouldn't matter because there would be hundreds of cuts and could be worked on in the edit. But when I saw the actors rehearsing for the master shot on set and I saw how Choi Min-sik (**03**) moved his body and how he got exhausted after going through the whole thing, it inspired me. I asked myself, why make a cartoon-like action sequence when it's not a fight where he's trying to get anything out of it? He is just trying to get out of there, so it's a meaningless fight really. Making such elaborate work of the scene would be art for art's sake, style for style's sake, so I decided to emphasize the sense of exhaustion and solitude in the one man fighting against great odds."

Park laughs that he finds action sequences "bothersome" to shoot, and he could have just shown the protagonist facing the sea of thugs and then cut to the next scene with his cut and bruised face, and the thugs all lying on the ground. "But you can't tell a story like that," he insists, "so I came up with the tableau idea. Only problem with this shot was that in the preceding shot, I had shown just how narrow the corridor was. But in the tableau shot, the distance from the wall and the camera makes the corridor seem much wider than it was established in the preceding shot. It doesn't make sense logically, but there are a great many sequences in the history of cinema where filmmakers intentionally ignore logic." By objectifying the protagonist in this way, Park serves to isolate him further. "It's a distancing effect, if you like. Rather than have the audience really identify with the character and find it cathartic when his fist first connects with a thug or hurt when he hurts, I wanted the audience to step away from the action and watch it from a distance." Visually he was inspired by the old European pastime of enacting famous paintings (tableau vivant). "The idea was that the sequence would be a moving version of that," he says. "It would be like a mural of a historical battle. And rather than using shorter weapons like daggers, I wanted them to use something longer to be reminiscent of soldier's pikes." The sequence was shot in one take, although "it took us a couple of days to get the best take."

"In filmmaking, everything is by design. There is no one element that is not and whether you think it's good taste or bad taste, everything is determined by the filmmaker's choice."

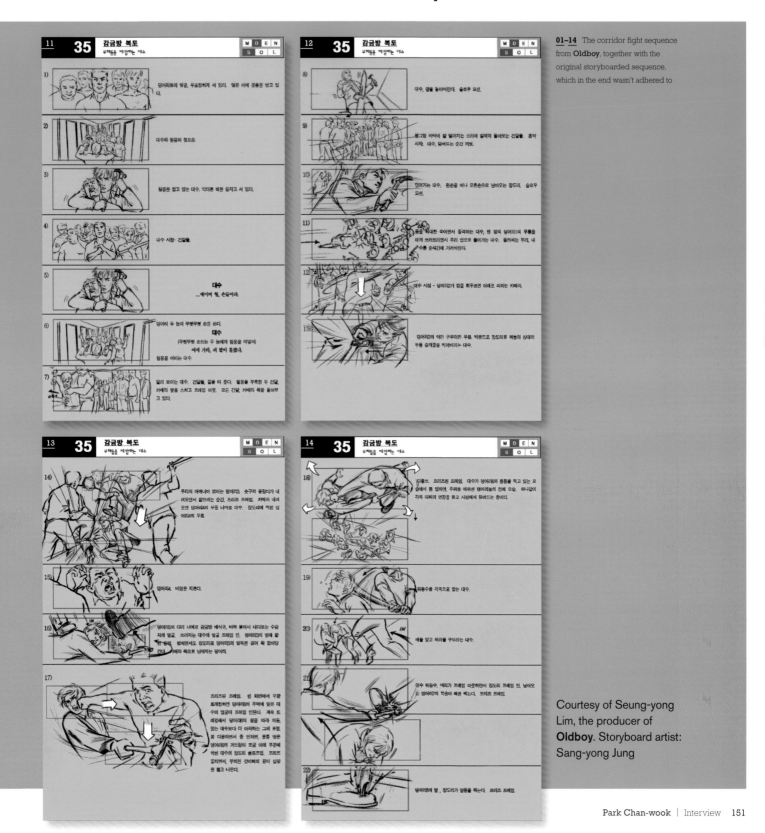

01–14 The corridor fight sequence from **Oldboy**, together with the original storyboarded sequence, which in the end wasn't adhered to

Courtesy of Seung-yong Lim, the producer of **Oldboy**. Storyboard artist: Sang-yong Jung

SYMPATHY FOR MR. VENGEANCE

Each of the films in the so-called "Vengeance" trilogy is different and indeed only the third film—**Lady Vengeance**—was consciously made as part of a trilogy.

Sympathy for Mr. Vengeance (01) started out with the idea of abducting a child, which, if it goes wrong, could become the worst crime a person could commit. "But if the outcome is a success for the abductor," says Park, "is it such a bad thing? That was the question I was asking myself. As long as the kid comes back to the parents, what's the harm in parting with a bit of money to ensure that your child comes back safely, especially if they are rich to begin with? In reality, of course, it rarely ends happily, but what if somebody found himself in dire circumstances and he was trying to come up with a crime that would have the least effect on anybody and the only crime he comes up with is to abduct a child. He believes he can take care of the child and return the child in exchange for money."

The film is essentially in two halves, the first about the abductor, the second about the father of the child who has died in an accident. "It creates confusion in the audience as to who to root for," he says. "They have spent the entire first half of the film empathizing with the protagonist, the deaf mute abductor, but at the exact mid-point of the film, when the child dies, the story is told from the father's perspective. And now the audience has to watch somebody who wants to kill the person they have been rooting for. The aim was to question the notion in thriller films of whose side you are on. Who do you root for?"

stage I am filled with ideas of how to do the film and it's quite exhilarating. I run at full steam until it ends.

I wrote the entire script for **Sympathy for Mr. Vengeance** in just two days. I had the film's complete structure in my head and once I sat down to write it, I was able to write the whole thing in one go without any trouble. Then again, it was a film without much dialogue and the leading character is a deaf mute, so that helped.

I like to thoroughly storyboard every single frame of the film in the manner you would see on screen, so the storyboard is like the edited film in a way. The reason I do that goes back to **JSA**. The film company who hired me couldn't really trust me because I had made these two failures, so at the start of the process, they put it in my contract to storyboard **JSA** so they could see what I

envisioned before going into production. It was a positive experience for me, however, and I have done it on every film ever since.

The storyboarding is an ongoing process before shooting starts: sometimes what we find in location scouting can inform the storyboard and sometimes the storyboard influences where we scout for locations; likewise with costumes, makeup and everything else, although it never dictates casting.

I shoot and edit almost exactly to the storyboard. There are minor changes depending on the production, but I have spent a lot of time imagining every shot in advance so there is really not that much to change. I don't like spending time on set discussing angles or camera position, I would rather spend that time talking with actors. There are instances where I shoot differently from

LADY VENGEANCE

(02–03) This film was created by Park to complete the "Vengeance" trilogy, and was designed to involve the audience. "At the start of the third act, the protagonist is about to carry out the vengeance, but she realizes that she is not worthy, that there are other people to whom she should hand over the vengeance on this perpetrator, and she basically directs the set-up for them. She finds the location, she sets everything out, she gets the cast of families together and watches as they take their revenge. She becomes a producer, a writer, a production designer and a director of this act of vengeance—and finally, she becomes the audience. When she buttons her leather trenchcoat to the top, it only reveals her eyes. I thought it was a fitting coda to the trilogy."

the storyboard [see **Oldboy** pages 149–151], but they are rare.

Collaborating with the actors is the biggest joy I get out of filmmaking because everything else is planned during pre-production. The only thing that remains a variable on set is an actor's performance and that keeps me on edge in a good way. Acting is a craft I have never learned and, even though I've worked as a director for many years, I still don't know how they do it. I am very respectful of actors, and if you think you see good performances from the actors in my films, it's probably a testament to my admiration for them.

The interesting thing about the post-production process is that, while you don't have the fun of working and playing with the actors, you have more time to yourself to experiment with things at your own pace. Music is something I enjoy the most during the post-production process. Sometimes the music can be in keeping with the emotion of a scene, or it can be jarring in an ironic way. In either case, this needs to be done in a very meticulous manner. Thanks to digital technology, which wasn't around when I first started, you can sync the music to the images frame by frame in a very delicate and specific manner.

It's immensely interesting to me to sit down with the music supervisor or composer and talk about what instruments they will use and what style the music will be, and talk about how they are going to approach it frame by frame and note by note. Creating the world of sound through sound effects, music, and silence is understandably very rewarding. →

THIRST

(01–06) Thirst is a film that Park had been developing for a decade or more and is perhaps his most contemplative film to date. "If it feels contemplative, it's because the priest reflects a lot more about my own personality than any other in my films," he explains. "Especially in the scene where the priest bursts into the bathroom to confront his illicit lover and goes on a diatribe, he talks nonsense like I do. And when he finds himself a vampire and is forced to adapt to the situation yet still struggles to live a good life even though he is a vampire, I think it's similar to how I deal with things in life."

The humor in the film is also telling and reflects a broader use of humor in Park's films to elicit thought in his audiences. "At the end, when the female protagonist scrambles under the car to avoid daylight and so survives, the priest rolls the car away and we find her hiding **(01–04)**. So at first, it's funny and the audience may laugh, but then they realize almost immediately how desperate the situation is for these people and even feel guilty at their own initial reaction. This duality of how one situation can be humorous and tragic at the same time, how humor is always infused with another emotion such as fury or sadness, fascinates me. This is why I sprinkle dark humor into the films." **(01–04)** Courtesy of Park Chan-wook. Storyboard artist: Conti Brothers (team name), Zoohan Cha (lead artist).

Of course, there is always an element of compromise in filmmaking, even though I try to avoid it. You are working with so many different people on a film and often with such a large budget that you have a responsibility, and I sometimes find myself in situations that aren't ideal. It's hard not to compromise literally.

Does that mean all my films are a result of compromise? I don't know, but if I had it my way, if I had complete freedom, my films would have been wilder. They would ignore traditional storytelling structure and logic a bit more, and you would see more violence and sex, and absurd humor in them. But then, reality is never the same as your dream situation and, if I were honest, I might not have the courage to be as free as I would like if I were given the opportunity. People already say I push my audience to the limits, so I am afraid of going further.

I do like to engage in a dialogue with the audience. I like to stimulate the audience so that they think about what they are watching. I want to provoke them and kick-start an intellectual process in their minds, and in order to do that I need to provoke them emotionally. People say that emotion and intellect don't go hand in hand, but I don't believe that is the case. It's not through philosophical dialogue that the audience members start to look back on themselves and question their world, but through emotional stimulation. Only by thinking why you are going through certain emotions watching what's happening on screen are you able to question what you are seeing.

The visual style has to work with that process. Visual style can never be style for style's sake. It should be the most effective and accurate way to create that emotional stimulus. In filmmaking,

everything is by design. There is no one element that is not and whether you think it's good taste or bad taste, everything is determined by the filmmaker's choice. Whether to do a long shot or a close-up, whether to use a blue cup instead or a red one? Many filmmakers—and I include myself in that—would not be able to give you an answer on the spot as to why they want a blue cup instead of a red one. It might just be a case of "I feel it's right." But after the film is done and you go back to revisit it, you will see that was the right choice.

The director always has his film in mind so that what they subconsciously can only describe as being the right choice at the time, can in hindsight turn out to having meaning or connection to the other elements of the film. For me this is the artist's training: rather than being able to intellectually articulate every choice that you make, you train yourself so that what you like is what is right.

Advice to young filmmakers

"Now we live in a day and age where, unlike when I first started out in the film business, digital technology enables you to make films even if you don't have the money, even if you don't have hundreds of people working on your film. So no longer can you use the excuse that you have talent, but don't have the resources. Now we live in an age where you can shoot a film with your iPhone and upload it to YouTube and see what you've done. So that old excuse doesn't apply to the new generation anymore."

István Szabó

"The close-up is everything. To me it's the
unique thing in filmmaking, telling the story
on a living human face with emotions that
change in front of an audience."

Hungarian master István Szabó graduated as a film director from the Academy of Drama and Film Art in Budapest in 1961 and directed six well-received short films before his acclaimed feature debut **The Age of Daydreaming**, which he made in 1964. His second film, **Father** (1966), secured his international standing, winning prizes at Moscow and Locarno, and set the tone for much of Szabó's future work, dealing as it does with the impact of Europe's totalitarian regimes on individuals.

Love Film (1970), **25 Fireman Street** (1973), **Budapest Tales** (1977) and the award-winning **Confidence** (1980) were standout films, but Szabó's finest work came in the early 1980s with three consecutive films starring Austrian stage actor Klaus Maria Brandauer—**Mephisto** (1981), **Colonel Redl** (1985), and **Hanussen** (1988). A trilogy of sorts about the compromises imposed on men in times of social, political and cultural turmoil, the films vaulted him to the top ranks of European auteurs. He won an Oscar for best foreign-language film for **Mephisto** and nominations for **Colonel Redl** and **Hanussen**.

Szabó's international fame led to English-language work in the 1990s and 2000s, including the lighter comic pieces **Meeting Venus** (1991) and **Being Julia** (2004). But he still occasionally makes a film in Hungarian, such as the powerful **Sweet Emma, Dear Bobe** (1992), and **Relatives** (2006).

And his preoccupation with history can be reflected in his three-hour opus **Sunshine** (1999), which spans three generations in one family, and **Taking Sides** (2001), which revisited the conflict between art and Nazism that he first brought to life in **Mephisto**.

His latest film, **The Door** (2012), is based on the novel by Magda Szabó and stars Helen Mirren and Martina Gedeck.

István Szabó

"At the beginning it was very important for me to make short films and even when I was making features, I did some shorts because they gave me an opportunity to experiment with different styles. For example, between **Budapest Tales** and **25 Fireman Street**, I did a short film called **Dream About a House** (1972), which involved one long shot down the lens. I wanted to try out this kind of photography to see how it worked.

I got the opportunity to make a feature film after having some success with my first short films. I was 25 and I wrote the screenplay very fast, and my energy was at such a high level that I had no questions and no fear. I went to battle and killed everybody. I shouted at everybody and did terrible things to show that I was the director. Of course, at that time I thought that directing a film meant you had to have everything in your hand. The poor actors had to do what I wanted to see and I did every shot a hundred times. It was crazy.

In that film, I had a lot of things to say, but I didn't have the technique to say them. That film has a lot of problems. In my second film, **Father**, the story was a little bit teenager-ish, but the energy of the message and my knowledge of filmmaking came together in a good way. I think it's my favorite film. It was very important for me to tell the story and it came from my heart, but I also, inadvertently, found my form.

As you get older, your knowledge about filmmaking, and even your vanity to show how good you are as a filmmaker, can get in the way of the story. At the beginning, it's the opposite: the idea and the message are far greater than your knowledge about filmmaking.

Decades later, you see the world differently and you have learned a lot along the way. The funny thing is that even though you think you are making different films, and I've heard it from a lot of directors, perhaps you are always making the same film. Everybody has a problem they want to address. It can be a personal issue or it can be a problem thrown at you by history or the people you are living around. But everyone has

01

something important to address immediately. I think in my case, I was born in middle Europe and I live in middle Europe and middle Europe has suffered a lot over the last century and has survived many political and historical changes, not just in my generation but in the generation of my parents and grandparents. So I think the most important problem faced by every character in my films is finding a feeling of security, not just a feeling of personal security, but also a safe future for their talent. So that could be the actor in **Mephisto** or one of the best officers in the army in **Colonel Redl** or the conductor Dr. Wilhelm Furtwängler in **Taking Sides**. The feeling of security is a composition of a lot of things depending on the character.

In all of middle Europe, be it Hungary or Slovakia or the Czech Republic or Poland or even part of Austria, people have similar difficulties. Looking back after forty years of making films, this was the most important theme. So yes, I wrote a lot of my films, but the screenplays I liked from other people also dealt with characters that had similar problems.

01 Szabó's second film, and one that he describes as his "favorite film," **Father**

SUNSHINE

(02–04) **Sunshine** is the epic story of a Hungarian Jewish family throughout the 20th century and features Ralph Fiennes (02–04) playing three different men in the family, first in the crumbling Austro-Hungarian empire, then in the Nazi holocaust, and finally in the new Communist regime of Hungary. It shot for a mammoth 114 days and the large cast included Jennifer Ehle (02, seen here with Szabó and Fiennes), Rosemary Harris, William Hurt, Rachel Weisz, and Deborah Kara Unger.

"I think we had Sundays off," laughs Szabó. "I got through it. It gives you enormous energy to do a film and you can stand for ten, twelve hours a day without a problem. But when it finishes, you collapse and get a cold, and develop stomach and back problems." (04) Szabó with Ralph Fiennes and cinematographer, Lajos Koltai.

Over the years you realize that filmmaking is not so complicated if you ask the right talented people to join you, people who can do their jobs and people you can trust. You tell them what you need and they do it. If they disagree with me, they tell me their idea and more often than not it's better than mine, which makes me sad because I feel so stupid.

There are two things that I learned through the years. First, I let go of my male vanity years ago. I don't care where the ideas come from, only that I need better ideas than I have and I am very thankful for them. I make a point of telling everyone loudly that this man or this woman had the idea. It's not enough just to accept good ideas from other people; they have to know that you appreciate it.

Second, what I have learned is that I love people very much. I have worked with the same people for many years. I have worked with the same makeup artist, wardrobe mistress and assistant director since **Mephisto**—that's more than thirty years. It's like a family.

As for the actors, they feel that I think they are the best people for the roles. It's important to me that they can try everything on the set because they know I am behind the camera. If it's too much, I tell them to tone it down. If it's not expressive enough or intense enough, I will ask for a little bit more. If I have a problem, I will →

tell them. But they can try everything because I need their freedom. That freedom is a little limited because we have to know exactly what we are doing and in what direction we are going, but they need to know that they can try. If their way of doing something is better than my idea, I will accept it. Of course, I have an opinion about everything in the film before we start.

Two months before the first day of shooting, I sit down around a big table with the heads of department—about twenty people from lighting to costume to props—and I take them through the script from page one, scene by scene, explaining everything I would like to do and asking questions about how we are going to do it. Because we are all together, people hear what other people are answering and how they are reacting and that can help solve problems or throw up other ideas.

When the actors are all cast, we read the screenplay together aloud and analyze every sentence so that there are no questions about what each sentence means. If I've written the script, I am absolutely flexible with the words. If the script is based on a novel, it's more difficult because I need to respect the writer. But I know that some expressions are good for one actor but not for another. So if actors don't like the words or the expressions, then we try to change them. Sometimes we take lines out. Or sometimes they will tell me they can't express what they need to with one line, and can I write something else to add to it.

I recently made a film with Helen Mirren based on a novel, which she really liked as well as the screenplay. And several times she wasn't happy with a line in the screenplay, so we changed it. We changed it only because Helen explained why and she is clear and clever, and I accepted that immediately.

Occasionally we will rehearse. In **Being Julia**, with Annette Bening, we rehearsed some of the very dramatic scenes before shooting. Rehearsals like that only occur if we want to develop a scene. It usually takes place when they come in for costume fittings and makeup tests.

01

I ask the actors to have two or three free days two weeks before shooting. It's an important time because when they are wearing the costumes, they know exactly what kind of character they have to play. In Helen Mirren's case, for example, it was when she had seen a specific pair of shoes for her character. She asked for a specific pair of shoes and as she took two or three steps in the shoes, she said "Fine, I know the character." She already had the character in her head of course, but this was the icing on the cake.

Every day of shooting, I have a morning meeting with my heads of department. It's called the cappuccino meeting. We talk about the challenges and problems of the shooting day. I tell them the shots and what I would like to achieve before shooting starts, and then indicate what's important for the following day. So they know everything about the day ahead and what I will expect the next day. It doesn't mean that we cannot change things, of course, because we always change things, but they know the main direction and they won't need to be asking questions about what's going on. That information is very important. If people are informed and know what is going on, they can come up with good ideas. If people are always coming up to me and asking questions, I will answer, but I am not responsible for my answers because I am focused on the shooting.

It is my job to have everything mapped out in my head for the scenes ahead of time. I get some basic ideas for each scene in the →

01 Annette Bening on stage in **Being Julia**

04 Klaus Maria Brandauer in **Hanussen**

05 Klaus Maria Brandauer with Szabó on the set of **Hanussen**

COLONEL REDL

(02–03) The highly charged final scenes of **Colonel Redl** see Redl instructed to commit suicide on trumped-up charges of treason. The final powerful scene sees Redl, as played by Klaus Maria Brandauer (**02, 03** with Szabó), left alone in his chambers after being handed the gun and pacing up and down frantically in despair and panic before putting the gun to his forehead.

But Szabó explains that was not how it was originally written. "We had Redl standing in front of a mirror and we watch him lifting his cap to shoot himself. But it wasn't moving, it wasn't good enough. Even Klaus couldn't express what he wanted to do and he was running up and down on the set with his stupid gun because he wanted to find something to do and I was standing there watching. We were alone on set. And I told him to stop running up and down, and that this was the scene. So we shot it like that. To be honest I think the idea came from Klaus' body. Klaus' body told us what to do. My job only was to tell Klaus that his body was running up and down the room and that was the movement we needed. Actors' instinct is one of the most important things," smiles Szabó, "and often even they do not know why they are doing something. They try and find emotion and the emotions often express themselves through movement. After **Mephisto**, I had 100 percent trust in Klaus' instinct."

KLAUS MARIA BRANDAUER

(01) Austrian Klaus Maria Brandauer starred in Szabó's trilogy, kicking off with **Mephisto** in 1981. Szabó describes him as "an enormously talented actor. For someone to carry a film, you need a charismatic person, and without a charismatic leading character, you don't have a film."

When he knew he needed a German-speaking actor for the film, he went to Berlin and was given the names of six actors to consider. "Without saying one word, I went to visit theaters in Germany and Austria, and saw the six actors perform. I saw Klaus perform and afterwards asked him for an appointment and we sat down and he agreed to a camera test. Gustaf Gründgens, on whom the character is based, was a very famous German actor and theater director who was actually very different from Klaus. His face and character and style of acting were different. To me what was important was the power and charismatic energy that Klaus possessed."

When Szabó was editing **Mephisto**, he invited Brandauer to visit the cutting room. "He saw the first edited version and said that I had edited the film with love, which meant that he liked it very much and what I used from his performance. And then he said that it would be nice to do another film together. I was thinking about what the subject could be and I thought we could find something that combined his Austrian blood and my Hungarian, which is how I arrived at **Colonel Redl**."

writing stage, but the final details come when I have seen locations, and the cinematographer and I have had long analytical discussions.

You have to be precise. For example, in Annette's scenes on stage in **Being Julia**, we rehearsed for two weeks. We had to know exactly what was going on because she was performing in front of an audience of 700 extras. But I couldn't have 700 extras for three days because of the expense involved; I could only have them for one day. So we had to do the shots first from this side and only this side and then later do the shots with the audience in them. The work sometimes demands incredible technical knowledge.

The same thing happened in the Olympic Games fencing sequence in **Sunshine**. You can't have a huge audience of extras for several shooting days—it would cost a fortune. So we had to know exactly how to use the extras over the course of a few days—1,000 on the first day,

300 on the second day, only 100 on the third day. So I made a landscape for my colleagues with all the shots. The shots would be color coded red for the first day with 1,000 extras, then blue for the second and green for the third. We kept this next to the camera and the crew knew exactly what we were going to do and when.

It's like building a house: you have to know where you need the water, how to build in the electricity.

There are three different movements in the creation of film. First is the screenplay, the final version of the screenplay, because you have to know what you want to say and how. Second is the shooting, but the shooting only creates material for the third, which is the editing room and that to me is the most important part because that's when you select what to use. For every shot, you have five or six or seven different versions, definitely a minimum of three. I never do a scene only once because it can happen that the scene gets destroyed or damaged in the lab. It happened to me on my third film, so I always insist that we do a minimum of three takes. Sometimes actors ask me and I say "it's for the lab." Sometimes the best work of an actor is not the take that is best for the film, or the opposite. Sometimes you can use two or three different parts from different takes. I can mix everything up. The editing room is a fantastic, beautiful place.

I've made films with many characters in them and I've made films with just two or three. To me they are no different. I learned from conversations with Ingmar Bergman and the films of Dreyer, Ozu and Bergman that the close-up is everything. To me it's the unique thing in filmmaking, telling the story on a living human face with emotions that change in front of an audience. Everything else is painting, describing, telling and it's a little superficial, but a really good close-up is unique. You cannot write it down.

So I do everything that is important for a film around those close-ups, but I concentrate on the faces of the actors. I could even tell you film history based on faces. If I name titles, you will remember faces. **Ivan the Terrible** (1976), **Citizen Kane** (1941), **Breathless** (1983), **Ashes and Diamonds** (1958). If the whole film is based on faces and they express something, they can represent the audience. Actors give the film its energy. They are the locomotives of the message. They share their feelings with the audience. **"**

Advice to young filmmakers

"Everybody is different and everybody's film is different, every actor is different, every story is different. If I can give advice, then my advice is what I learnt, that in filmmaking the only unique thing is a living human face with emotions. The audience has to care about the faces that appear on screen because the audience is represented by those faces. But the face belongs to an actor. I love actors. Oh, and be nice to the crew. There are a lot of people who can tell stories sitting in a coffee shop, but to make a film, you need people on your side. Without the crew, you cannot do a film."

02–03 **Taking Sides** starring Stellan Skarsgård and Harvey Keitel

Peter Weir

"In some of my films, I attempt to show how vast, unknowable and interesting the world is because it's the way it used to feel to me. From living at the bottom of the world in 1965, the world felt huge and you would only see Paris in movies."

Peter Weir first made a name as part of the Australian film renaissance of the 1970s alongside other directors like Fred Schepisi, Bruce Beresford and Phillip Noyce. After a decade working in sketch comedy and television, and making documentaries and shorts, he made his feature debut in 1974 with **The Cars That Ate Paris**, followed by the international hit **Picnic at Hanging Rock** in 1975 and supernatural thriller **The Last Wave** (1977). After making a modest TV movie, **The Plumber** in 1979, he made more international waves with the classic war epic **Gallipoli** (1981), starring Mel Gibson, who also led the cast in **The Year of Living Dangerously** (1982), a drama set against the turmoil of the 1965 presidential coup in Indonesia.

Inevitably Weir had attracted the attention of Hollywood and he made the move with the celebrated thriller **Witness** (1985), which won Oscar nominations for Best Picture, Best Director and for Harrison Ford for Best Actor. Ford also starred in Weir's **The Mosquito Coast** in 1986, based on the novel by Paul Theroux.

Weir's lucid storytelling, visual confidence and confident embrace of large themes worked wonders with his next film, **Dead Poets Society** (1989), a potentially conventional studio tearjerker that he transformed into a mainstream blockbuster that tapped into a spiritual zeitgeist around the world. It won Oscar nominations for Best Picture and Weir's second for Best Director.

After a well-liked experiment with romantic comedy **Green Card** (1990), which scored him an Oscar nomination for best original screenplay, Weir made one of his most ambitious dramas, **Fearless** (1993), about the survivors of an air crash. Although a disappointment at the box office, it has a dedicated following twenty years after its first release. Since 1993, Weir has made only three films— **The Truman Show** (1998) starring Jim Carrey, a mainstream critical and commercial hit, which won him his third directing Oscar nomination; **Master and Commander: The Far Side of the World** (2003), based on the Patrick O'Brian novels, which won a Best Picture Oscar nomination; and **The Way Back** (2010), a sweeping drama about a group of prisoners in a Russian gulag who escape during World War II and make an epic trek from Russia to India.

Peter Weir

" I grew up going to the movies as a kid on Saturday afternoons, but unlike many of my American contemporaries who knew that film was going to be their world, I had no idea what I was going to do. Then, when I was 20, I went to Europe in the way many young Australians did and still do. When I went, it was more of an adventure because we went by ship and that journey—five weeks at sea—set me on this path because I got involved in the ship's revue. There was a closed-circuit TV on the ship, which had never been used, and we asked the entertainments officer if we could use that to do a comedy show. So by the time I got off the ship at Athens, I knew that I wanted to do something in the area of acting or writing.

I got to London planning to get a job in theater, and I did, selling tickets! I kept on writing and did a little sketch comedy on amateur night at The Troubadour Club with friends from the ship. Back in Australia, I carried on working with my friends on revue shows and made a couple of short films funded by the government short-film fund.

On my second trip to London in 1970, on a study grant from the government film fund, I decided to concentrate on film and settle in Australia. My generation was the first that decided to come back as opposed to remaining in London. My first script **The Cars That Ate Paris** was accepted by the government feature film fund and I was very fortunate to be synchronous with the emergence of this fund.

My first feature was an overwhelming experience. I had set myself the goal of making a feature before I was thirty, as I felt that if I didn't get going before that age I wouldn't have that chance again. The film opens with what looks like an advertisement for cigarettes, with a good-looking couple in a sports car out in the countryside, and they have an accident and are killed. So you can see the sketch comedy influence! I'd grown up with the Hammer horror films and the town of secrets in the film fits in with that kind of tradition.

Having been a performer on stage and in my short films, I had a great rapport with actors. I

01 Jeff Bridges as Max Klein

02 Reference material used by Weir for the film

03 A drawing by an eight-year-old extra on the film

FEARLESS

(01–03) One of Weir's most intriguing films, **Fearless**, written by Rafael Yglesias, explored the lives of plane crash survivors and the script used as its starting point the real-life crash of United 232 in 1989. "That was an interesting experience," says Weir. "My key research was meeting a remarkable group of people who had been on that DC-10. Five or six survivors agreed to talk to me on condition that they would be frank about the details of the awfulness and horror of what they saw. So I had these interesting conversations at night during the preparation of the film and altered the script accordingly."

As a result of the conversations, Weir took out all exterior shots of the accident, and made them first-person subjective views from the cabin. "In a way, the most important part in what they told me was the dreamy quality of it. They told me how the brain clicked into a sort of slow motion and strange little things they saw like someone reaching out for a hand or a strange light."

01

> "The cutting room is like the final writing stage, although you do it in a different way and you've got a finite amount of material, but an infinite number of ways to combine that material. I think if it's got a spark, the spark's always going to be there."

thought that acting and writing would be my career for a period. The directing really came quite late, and because we had no industry in Australia at the time, you didn't grow up at the feet of giants. While on the one hand that was hard because we had no one to inspire us, at the same time we had nothing to beat or overcome. We were the first.

It was a lucky period for a young filmmaker in Australia. We were all on the starting blocks together, and I could think of twenty other promising directors who didn't come through. I think some people ran out of steam, they didn't have a feel for it. I think it was just natural to me somehow. I must have absorbed it through the pores of my skin from going to those Saturday afternoon movies as a child. You learnt the grammar like a child learns a foreign language—very quickly.

I always think of the audience. I think it goes back to performing when we did those live shows. My co-writer and I would write the sketches together and if the audience was with you, we'd expand the sketch and conversely if the audience wasn't responding, you'd tighten it up or lean more toward the slapstick. I think I got to really feel an audience and, as difficult as it is for a filmmaker, preview audiences can help you with the film. I can feel them through that old mechanism of being on stage and I can make a lot of adjustments in the cutting room as a result of those feelings.

I felt that I became confident with what I was doing on my third feature **The Last Wave**, which in my own private university was some sort of graduation film. Before that, I could analyze why something hadn't worked, but I found it very difficult to work out why something had worked that I'd not planned. Why did the audience get caught up in that particular part of the film? Sometimes it's a collision of elements that you can pick apart and try to understand. That is part of learning on the job, I guess.

To an extent, I think I know what will work and what won't now. There are always moments →

THE TRUMAN SHOW

(01–06) For Weir, it was clear when he first took on **The Truman Show** that there was only one actor who could play the leading role: Jim Carrey. "Tom Hanks could have done it, but he was ruled out early on because he'd done **Forrest Gump**, and Jim was always interested. I had seen him in **Ace Ventura: Pet Detective** (1994) and I thought he was remarkable. We met and got on immediately and began inventing things from the first moment."

Carrey, however, wasn't available for nine months and producer Scott Rudin suggested that Weir meet other actors. "I told him we should wait for Jim. I couldn't see anybody else doing it and it was a long, long wait."

Once on set, Weir found that Carrey needed to go through a process of relinquishing control. "I think he'd always directed himself really prior to working with me and I found that difficult the first couple of weeks because we'd do a take and he would come round and want to watch it and come up with new ideas. And I would say that we had what I needed. So I had a talk with him about it and said that he had to trust me to say we've got the shot. And he found that difficult. And I said that's what I do, that's the way I have grown as a director. Then I had an inspiration: Truman doesn't know he's on television, but the more you look at the monitor, the more likely you are to fall out of character. So I said he shouldn't look at the monitor again. He was coming to watch dailies anyway, so he knew what I was printing. After a couple of weeks, he just let me do my job." (**01**) Weir with Jim Carrey on set. (**05–06**) Storyboards for the film drawn by Peter Weir.

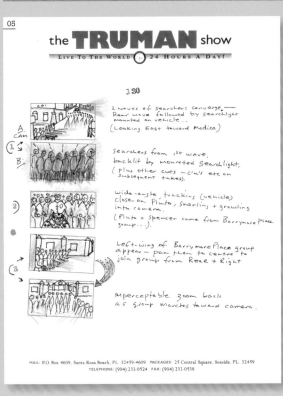

the **TRUMAN** show
LIVE TO THE WORLD 24 HOURS A DAY!

130

2 waves of searchers converge—
Rear wave followed by searchlight
mounted on vehicle...
(Looking East toward Medica)

Searchers from 1st wave,
backlit by mounted Searchlight.
(plus other cuts — clu's etc on
subsequent takes).

Wide-angle, tracking (vehicle)
close on Pluto, snarling + growling
into camera.
(Pluto + Spencer come from Barrymore Place
group...).

Left-wing of Barrymore Place group
appear — pan them to centre to
join group from Rear + Right

Imperceptable zoom back
as group marches toward camera.

MAIL: P.O. Box 4609, Santa Rosa Beach, FL 32459-4609 PACKAGES: 25 Central Square, Seaside, FL 32459
TELEPHONE: (904) 231-0524 FAX: (904) 231-0538

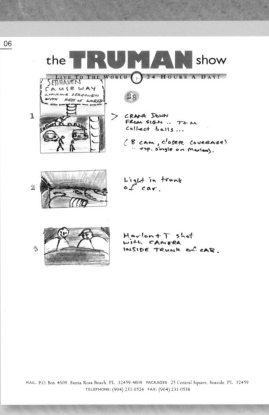

the **TRUMAN** show
LIVE TO THE WORLD 24 HOURS A DAY!

SEAHAVEN
CAUSEWAY
LINKING SEAHAVEN
WITH REST OF WORLD

28

CRANE DOWN
FROM SIGN .. T+M
collect balls...
(B cam, closer coverage)
... esp. single on Marlons.

Light in trunk
of car.

Marlon + T shot
WITH CAMERA
INSIDE TRUNK of CAR.

MAIL: P.O. Box 4609, Santa Rosa Beach, FL 32459-4609 PACKAGES: 25 Central Square, Seaside, FL 32459
TELEPHONE: (904) 231-0524 FAX: (904) 231-0538

WITNESS

(01–02) This was Weir's first US studio movie and what could have been a routine cop thriller became transcendent in his hands, winning multiple Oscar nominations including Best Picture, Director and Actor for Harrison Ford **(01)**. "I don't know what I think about that film now," he says. "It seemed such a slight piece at the time. I've had people tell me that it comes up on TV and they don't intend to watch it, but they get sucked into it. There's something strangely soothing about it, I think. Something in the mood and the music."

He had been offered a US film by Warner Bros. after **Picnic At Hanging Rock**, but turned it down. "I didn't feel a great rapport with the material, but more importantly I didn't feel I was ready to do that and was enjoying what I was doing in Australia. I thought, you can't go to Hollywood without knowing what you're doing, without being comfortable with the craft, you'd just get eaten alive. So I left it until 1984."

where a film won't connect with the public and you thought it would. You may never know why it has failed. But then again, it's quite fascinating how a film takes on a life of its own; this brings me to a well-used analogy, which is that the film is the child and you give birth to it and raise it, but you have to let it go. And as with a child, it takes on its own particular personality and at a certain point, you have to serve that. You have to drop that scene or do more of those scenes because the film needs it. A lot of this comes in the cutting room.

The cutting room is like the final writing stage, although you do it in a different way and you've got a finite amount of material, but an infinite number of ways to combine that material. I think if it's got a spark, the spark's always going to be there, but it's a case of making it as bright as you can. There is no way you can put that spark in if it's not in the material.

Perhaps I achieve a sense of "scale" in my films for a number of reasons: one was the tremendous impact of traveling to Europe in 1965, getting a sense of distance by traveling by ship, which was a gift I didn't realize at the time. Nowadays, of course, you can get anywhere within twenty-four hours. I think that trip gave me a feeling for adventure, for setting off on a journey, which is reflected in many of my films.

In some of my films, I attempt to show how vast, unknowable and interesting the world is because it's the way it used to feel to me. From living at the bottom of the world in 1965, the world felt huge and you would only see Paris in movies.

The other, quite different circumstance, was that in the early 1970s, very few of our actors in Australia could say dialogue and very few of us could write it. So I tended to delete dialogue and let the camera tell the story.

DEAD POETS SOCIETY

(03–04) After he had made **Witness**, Weir was approached to direct **Dead Poets Society**, a project that he initially felt was "too much of a melodrama" since the teacher John Keating (to be played by Robin Williams) originally suffered from cancer. "I only did the picture on the condition that I could take out the cancer storyline and it just fell out nicely."

Weir's relationship with Robin Williams also helped the film, he says. "That background of sketch comedy gave us a wonderful way of talking together because I could play the straight man with him, and just drop back into those early days when I was writing and performing."

He thinks the film's connection to young audiences and its enduring popularity today was a result of its lack of politics. "It was originally set in the 1960s in the era of rebellion, but I wanted it moved back to the 1950s. It's not about revolt against the bourgeois, it's more about what you make of yourself, what you are going to be and what art—or poetry in this case—can give you. I wasn't selling anything or pushing anything, there was no polemic, there was no sugar-coated message that I think young people can smell a mile away. And they responded to it because it was really saying life is what you make it."

Here's an example: you have two people in a café and the scene opens with the waitress bringing over coffee and she slops the coffee down and it spills into the saucer and she asks "You want something else?" That sets the scene into a bad mood. But when the actress couldn't say the lines because they just sound hopeless and amateurish, I told her not to say anything, just to put the coffee down. But I still want to show that this woman is very sloppy so I ask the wardrobe people to get a pair of rotten old slippers and we put a bandage with blood on it around her finger. So then I do a close-up of her feet flip-flopping across the floor, a close-up of the two people having coffee turning to see her approaching. One of them looks at her hand and I do a close-up on the bandage. She slops the coffee down and the two people move the coffees to one side.

In the early days, that was the kind of survival technique I would apply. I also loved silent movies and even to this day, I watch a couple of favorites before I make a movie just to re-educate myself in storytelling without synchronous sound.

Whenever I've written a script for an American studio or financier, or rewritten a script, which already has accredited writers, I'll drop dialogue. The executives in the US often find this puzzling, because the story isn't explicable without the dialogue and that's how they read a script: they read the dialogue and scan the descriptions, which are usually pretty basic. I tend to expand the descriptions and cut the dialogue.

I got into a tricky spot with my first American film **Witness**. At the end of that movie, the police detective played by Harrison Ford is leaving the farm to go back to his life in Philadelphia and he goes to say goodbye to the Amish woman. Their romance is clearly not going to go anywhere. You see him driving away and passing the Amish →

MASTER AND COMMANDER: THE FAR SIDE OF THE WORLD

(01–07) Weir has worked with many of the same collaborators over the years, including cinematographer Russell Boyd (07, with Peter Weir), who shot some of his earliest Australian movies, as well as **Master and Commander** and **The Way Back**, and editors Billy Anderson and Lee Smith. "They know what you like and you know what their capabilities are," says Weir. "I like to have contributions as long as those making them are comfortable with me saying no. Some people get a bit sensitive if they come up with an idea and you don't go with it. I like collaborators who are unafraid and confident enough to say an opposing idea to the one you have, but who are then quite comfortable if you don't choose it. It's not personal." (01–05) Building HMS *Surprise* and how she appeared onscreen. (06) Weir with Russell Crowe, who played Captain Jack Aubrey in the film.

man coming down the hill and you realize that she is going to have a life with him.

Originally there were two pages of dialogue in which Harrison explained why he was leaving and she gave her feelings to him. It was very literal, and I cut it all because we didn't need it. The producer told me that the studio would never accept it because we need to know what they are feeling. I knew that if I had done my job properly, you would know exactly how they were feeling by the time it was all cut together. They just look at each other. It's hopeless, it's beyond words.

The executive from the studio, Jeffrey Katzenberg, who was at Paramount at the time, flew out to talk to me and suggested I shoot it both ways just in case. That seemed a waste of time to me so Jeff asked me to paint a picture in words for him and tell it like a story. So, over coffee in this restaurant in Lancaster Pennsylvania, I told him. He thought it sounded fine.

Casting is interesting. You think you know what kind of actor you want to play a part and then you meet somebody who completely alters that perception. I did a TV movie in 1979 in Australia called **The Plumber** and there was the part of the plumber, who was a working-class guy, and a couple who were university graduates. The wife had been set so I auditioned husbands and plumbers, and I finished one audition with a very good actor for the husband, and he said he always gets the husband parts and would love to play the plumber. He auditioned and he was wonderful. I realized that I was casting in a clichéd way by casting actors who always play working-class types. By taking somebody who usually plays the middle-class type and putting them in the plumber's shoes, it brought something else. And he got the part. It was a wonderful lesson for me in the 1970s and I keep that slight recklessness in the casting period, as I think I do when I am shooting. I like the idea of a controlled situation, but you have to leave room for the wild or unexpected.

I pass that onto my casting directors so they

PICNIC AT HANGING ROCK

(01) Weir became bewitched by the novel **Picnic at Hanging Rock** by Joan Lindsay when it was brought to him as a potential directing project. "As a kid, I loved Sherlock Holmes, but the best part was always the set-up. I was always a bit disappointed when you finally got the explanation. But I was aware with **Picnic at Hanging Rock**, that it could be a disaster, because the audience would be waiting for an explanation at the end, and they wouldn't get one. So I had to create a mood within the picture in which you really didn't want an explanation, you really hoped it didn't come and you were also unsure what you wanted it to be. So that was an exercise in technique and craft in creating an ambience which was in itself haunting and odd and therefore you would accept that it was completely insoluble and that would be the pleasure."

To create the mood of unease, he shot close-ups, both normally as part of the coverage of the scene but also at different camera speeds. "I asked the actors not to blink during a scene so it would appear to be a conventional 24-frames-per-second shot, but it would actually be moving at a different speed." On the soundtrack, he also added effects to unsettle the audience. "I had read a theory that we carry in our DNA potential to be made uneasy by certain things and I thought an earthquake would be one of those things, so I took the sound effect of an earthquake and slowed it right down and buried it in the mix. It came out as a deep low growl but you couldn't be sure if it was the theater you were in or on the soundtrack of the film."

01

don't become too conservative and that resulted in casting director Dianne Crittenden coming up with the idea of Alexander Godunov to play the Amish man rival for the young woman's affections in **Witness**. I knew of him slightly from the press, but didn't think he was an actor. She said she had met him and he had charm and a wonderful smile. So we had him in and he couldn't really say dialogue very well, but he did have this charm that you could photograph.

You have to trust the actors and they have to trust you. I think that's what the first meetings are all about whether they be casting meetings or meeting a star for lunch or dinner. The verbal part of it is the least important aspect of the meeting. I think you sense somebody and they sense you. You have to see if there is a connection between your sensibilities. If there isn't that kind of unseen handshake, I don't think you will ever work well together.

When I was preparing **The Last Wave**, I wanted tribal Aboriginals in the film and in particular Nandjiwarra Amagula to play the tribal elder. I went to see him in Darwin where he was rehearsing some dances and my advisor said that I should just go up and sit with him and talk. He hadn't agreed to do the film yet, but he had been told the story broadly. So I went up and sat with him on a beach for four hours while he rehearsed, and we didn't say a word, but I began to feel like he was checking me out somehow. At the end of the day, he asked if he could bring his wife to the shoot. That was it. I had passed the audition, and it was a good lesson for me.

I think the most difficult times for me fall into two areas. As every filmmaker knows, time is the enemy during shooting because there just isn't enough time in the day and you've got to get the sequence today and the weather might not be what you want. But the practical side of it is dwarfed by the creative challenges, when you know something is not working or you're not reaching far enough for something. The challenges are always fundamentally creative. "

Casting female as male

(02) One of Weir's most famous casting decisions—and indeed one of cinema's most famous—was the choice of American actress Linda Hunt to play the Chinese–Australian male dwarf Billy Kwan opposite Mel Gibson in **The Year of Living Dangerously**.

"I was looking at short Asian actors and then short actors who could be made up Asian and we found an actor," he recalls. "But when we began rehearsing in Sydney with Mel [Gibson] it didn't go well and Mel said that the guy irritated him and he would never work with someone like this. We were only a couple of weeks from shooting in Manila, so I paid him off and went to LA and New York for replacement auditions. When Linda came in to read, it was a joke of sorts on the part of the casting director. I was reading Mel's lines and she was in front of me and I asked if she could play a man. We did a test and her female sensibility kind of made everything work. When I got back to the production office, Russell Boyd and all these other faces turned to me and said 'Did you get a Billy?' And I said 'Yes, and it's a woman.' So they asked if I was going to rewrite it as a woman. 'No, I said, she is going to play a man.' And there was silence."

And what did Mel Gibson say? "Not much," laughs Weir. "Not much at all. But after a little rehearsing with her and one day of shooting, he said this is going to work." Hunt won the Best Supporting Actress Oscar for her performance.

Zhang Yimou

"It's not easy. Every film is a long and difficult process and you need to have the passion for creation to be able to enjoy it."

China's greatest living filmmaker with eighteen films to his credit, Zhang Yimou started his directing career as one of the Fifth Generation of Chinese filmmakers with his first film **Red Sorghum** in 1987. This group of directors was the first to graduate from the Beijing Film Academy after the end of the Cultural Revolution and brought a bold and adventurous style of storytelling to Chinese cinema.

Zhang had graduated as a cinematographer and had already shot three films from Fifth Generation directors—Zhang Junzhao's **One and Eight** and Chen Kaige's **Yellow Earth** and **The Big Parade**—before switching to directing.

Immediately recognized on the international festival circuit, Zhang made film after film, which garnered critical acclaim and distribution deals around the world. Although he dismisses his second film, the thriller **Codename Cougar**, co-directed by Yang Fengliang, he went on to make **Ju Dou** (1990), **Raise the Red Lantern** (1991), **The Story of Qiu Ju** (1992), **To Live** (1994), **Shanghai Triad** (1995), **Keep Cool** (1997), **Not One Less** (1999), **The Road Home** (2000) and **Happy Times** (2000).

Famous for his diversity—he could make the simplest story about village folk followed by a lavish period piece about gangsters or emperors—Zhang achieved his biggest success with the martial arts epic **Hero** in 2002, which grossed over $175m around the world, including $53m in the US—extraordinary for a foreign-language film.

Since then, he has alternated between big budget and small pieces with **House of Flying Daggers** (2004), **Riding Alone for Thousands of Miles** (2005), **Curse of the Golden Flower** (2006), **A Woman, a Gun and a Noodle Shop** (2009), which was a Chinese remake of the Coen Brothers' **Blood Simple**, and **Under the Hawthorn Tree** (2010). At the time of going to press, he had just completed his biggest film to date, **The Flowers of War** (2011), a drama set against the Nanjing massacre and featuring Oscar winner Christian Bale.

Although he was out of favor with the Chinese government in the 1990s, he now works within the state film system and in 2008 he directed the opening ceremonies for the 2008 Olympic Games in Beijing.

Zhang Yimou

“ I majored in cinematography at the Beijing Film Academy and if I had followed the path of the state-owned film studio system, I would have ended up as a cinematographer working in one of the state-owned studios. In fact after graduating, I was assigned to Guangxi Film Studio.

But in my second year at film school, I decided that I wanted to change to become a director. At the time my goal wasn't very clear. I was the oldest student in my class, which was somewhat embarrassing, and when I looked at the director class, there were some older students like me so I thought I should join them because I wouldn't stand out so much with them.

Also at that time, I borrowed some textbooks about film directing. One was called **Grammar of the Film Language**, a very practical book, and one was about film editing. I remember reading those books secretly because I didn't want my classmates to know that I was considering changing.

I decided that I needed to make my mark in cinematography before switching to directing, my thinking being that if I couldn't be a good cinematographer, it wouldn't be convincing if I wanted to change to be a director. It was my personal ambition to make the change, but it was also related to the state system at the time. You had to have permission from the studio executives to change your position at the studio, or to move to another studio.

I was DoP on three films: **One and Eight** with director Zhang Junzhao and both **Yellow Earth** and **The Big Parade** with Chen Kaige. On those films, I learned about the entire process of making a film, from preparation, discussion, to shooting. At that time, there was a clear division of work between the different disciplines according to the rules of the industry, but we shared everything. It was all about teamwork and helping each other. It was much more like making big student films.

So after I had won some awards for **Yellow Earth**, I felt that I had gained approval from the industry that I was a good cinematographer and

decided that it was time to apply for permission to change to directing. The process may sound old-fashioned and rigid, but the good thing about it is that it makes sure you are really qualified as a filmmaker. The executive had to be responsible for his decision so we went through a strict process to qualify me. With the help of director Wu Tianming, who was the director of Xi'an Film Studio, I was transferred to Xi'an Film Studio as a guest film director. Of course, today anyone can be a director and you are free to work on any position in a film.

When I made my first film, **Red Sorghum**, I felt I had the natural passion of a young man, daring to say something out loud about his creativeness, to be different and innovative, to be myself. It is like a Chinese saying: newborn calves do not fear the wolves.

Actually I think I still have this kind of passion to make every new film of mine today. I don't feel that much different. It's just that, as I gained more experience along the way, I have more decisions to make these days.

It's not easy. Every film is a long and difficult process and you need to have the passion for creation to be able to enjoy it. I don't stop making films because I enjoy that process of creating something so much. But it's not always easy to make it happen.

After **Raise the Red Lantern**, I knew that I would be making films for the rest of my life. The first film was about passion for creation and a proclamation of myself as a filmmaker, and even though I won some awards, I was still not so sure. In the second film, I started to try different ways to tell stories. After three or four films, I had gained confidence in myself and confidence that I would be making different kinds of films for many years.

Almost every film of mine is adapted from existing novels or literary works. But the films are ultimately very different from the novels. I like to think of the process like the high jump or the long jump. The novel gives you a springboard and then you want to jump higher or longer. You want to jump differently and with your own style. Basically, that is how I do it. It has become a habit

"I always wanted to make films for the public, for the common man, and make the films enjoyable. I have never pretended to be a deep thinker."

of mine. There are a few films that were based on original screenplays like **Happy Times** and **Codename Cougar**, but they turned out to be unsuccessful. Because of them, I always look for good novels for the basis of my next project. Even though I still change the novel into something completely different, I would still look for an existing story.

It's usually a very long process to go from novel to script to being ready to shoot. I usually find a writer and talk to him about the book, trying to communicate my ideas about the adaptation and my vision for the film. This communication stage takes about two or three months. Then the writer needs at least six months to write the first draft; then I discuss the script with the writer and my producer, and we make revisions. If I am not happy with the script, we may have to find a new writer and start the whole process all over again. So the process can take two years. If I have to change two or three writers on one project, I give up on the project because of the time and money it costs.

Casting is one of the most important aspects of my films and it is something I am very proud of. I consider it a signature in my filmmaking. Through the years, we have developed a very scientific method to scour the country for the most suitable actors. For example, in **Not One Less**, we searched through villages and mobilized farmers and villagers to take part in the auditions. It took us a year and over 5,000 auditions to find the non-professional actor Wei Minzhi for the leading role. And for **Under the Hawthorn Tree**, we went through 6,000 young acting students to find Zhou Dongyu. We have a team of about ten people who go around the country taking video footage of every possible candidate and then one of my assistant directors who serves as casting director will look at the videos and I will make the final decision. This process needs to be done in a quiet and discreet manner, but my crew also needs to be very diligent and efficient.

I rehearse the actors, but not for specific scenes. I usually do what I call basic technique →

RED SORGHUM

(01) Zhang's first feature **Red Sorghum** starred Gong Li as a woman who takes over a wine distillery set among the fields of Sorghum in the eastern Chinese province of Shandong during the Second Sino-Japanese War in the late 1930s. Zhang still says it remains one of his favorite films "because it was my first film and because I remember that passion to create and the no-regrets attitude I had to work with the whole team."

It is based on a novel by Mo Yan and firmly established the director as one of the bright lights of the Fifth Generation of filmmakers.

"I have to be thankful to all the cast and crew members of **Red Sorghum**, but when I look back, the biggest help to me on my first film was the story. As Fifth Generation filmmakers, we had been growing as mature filmmakers alongside the renaissance in the literary world in the 1980s. At the time, the Cultural Revolution had just ended and there was a revival of contemporary literature in China. You could say that the common feature and artistic expression of the Fifth Generation filmmakers was that they all came from or were nurtured by the literature of the period. There was no filmmaking geniuses really: it was the literature that inspired us so much, and all the films of the Fifth Generation were adapted from the books of the 1980s. We really should be thankful to those authors. Today I feel even more grateful to them because a good story is so hard to find these days."

01

Colors

From the beautiful reds of **Raise the Red Lantern (01)** or **Shanghai Triad (07)** to the dazzling color palette of **Hero (03–04, 09)**, the gorgeous green of **House of Flying Daggers (05–06)**, and the excessive golds in **Curse of the Golden Flower (02, 08, 10)**, colors are a central part of Zhang's films.

"Color is always important in my films," he says. "I have a habit of using colors to help me tell the story, whether it's symbolic or poetic. I guess it's my obsession that I always prefer movies with rich colors. In **The Flowers of War**, I also use colors. It's the story of a choirgirl who always wore long dark blue skirts and whose world was bland and innocent until a group of prostitutes arrived at the church. Suddenly the world became brightly colored."

Collaboration with Gong Li

Zhang has worked with many celebrated actors on multiple occasions, but none more frequently than Gong Li, now one of Asia's most legendary stars whom he cast in her first role in **Red Sorghum** and subsequently in seven other films. Among other accolades, she won the best actress prize at Venice for **The Story of Qiu Ju**. Zhang and Gong were partners in real life until 1995, but continued to work together after their relationship ended.

"She is a very smart actor and has very strong instincts for her roles, which is something very valuable for actors," says Zhang. "She is never shy of expressing her opinion on the character and making suggestions about how she will play the character, which is always very helpful for me. Of course, when we started we made films like a big family: the team lived and worked together, and we discussed the film endlessly. Nowadays, I work with actors who have never worked with me before, but that is not important. The important thing is for the actor to be able to express his opinion on the character. Even with the young actors, I encourage them to tell me what they think about their roles."

01 The Story of Qui Ju

02 Ju Dou

03–04 Raise the Red Lantern

05 Curse of the Golden Flower

"I like to think of the process like the high jump or the long jump. The novel gives you a springboard and then you want to jump higher or longer. You want to jump differently and with your own style."

rehearsals, especially for young and inexperienced actors. I rehearse them for a long time. But with experienced actors, I rehearse them less. Usually we just talk about situations, feelings and ideas. Situational rehearsals are what I do when the actors need to experience the life of the character. For example, when an actor is going to portray a farmer or a village girl, you need to know what a farmer's life or village life is like. So you learn to ride a horse or farm the land or milk a cow.

We have also done a lot of actors' training for many of my films. On **The Flowers of War**, we did an unprecedentedly large amount of training for actors. We needed to train them to look like the girls who worked in brothels in the 1930s. They needed to learn how to dance, to get used

to wearing Qipaos, to play Chinese chess, to play musical instruments and to smoke elegantly. We invited an 80-year-old actress who had direct experience of the 1930s to teach the girls basic skills. Finally, we needed them to perform in English naturally. It was hard work. We trained thirty girls in total and worked for more than two years with the leading actress. That is the largest actor training program I've ever had on a film.

I usually talk straight to the point with my cinematographer. There are no wasted words about the atmosphere or mood I want to create because I know the technical aspects of creating the scene so I will direct them in technical and practical terms. For example, I would tell them not to use too much light in one scene and keep it simple in another. Even though I haven't →

TO LIVE

(06–08) Zhang's 1994 film **To Live**—an eloquent saga of three generations living through the turbulence of 20th-century Chinese history—won the Grand Jury Prize and the best actor prize for Ge You at the Cannes Film Festival, but it was banned in China for its portrait of government policy during the Cultural Revolution. Zhang was not permitted to attend Cannes, and was furthermore banned from filmmaking for two years afterwards.

"Censorship is something that has existed for a long time in China and there is not much a filmmaker can do about it because it exists within the current political system," he says. "One can only hope that the political system in the future can be more transparent and more democratic. This might take thirty years or fifty years or longer to happen, nobody knows. Maybe the next generation of filmmakers can finally enjoy complete freedom of creation. Under the current restrictions, we are not able to create films that dig so deep into human history or are strong in critical views of human nature. We can only hope that will change, while continuing to make movies as we can."

HERO / HOUSE OF FLYING DAGGERS

With his two ravishing martial arts films **Hero** (**01–03**) and **House of Flying Daggers** (**04–07**), Zhang entered the realm of box-office blockbusters, scoring success at home in China and internationally. Both were enormous productions of great spectacle and featured major stars—**Hero** starred Jet Li, Tony Leung, Maggie Cheung (**02**), Donnie Yen and Zhang Ziyi, while **House of Flying Daggers** featured Takeshi Kaneshiro, Andy Lau and Zhang Ziyi (**05** and **06–07** with Yimou).

"They were both very difficult to make," he says. "We wanted to make sure the action was working and also that the picture looked exactly as we had designed. Plus we wanted the weather and the wind to be right, and the water to flow in the way we wanted. It's not easy. There are also horses to wrangle and thousands of extras to handle. Sometimes you stick to the picture in your head and try your best to make the scene happen. But you also need to be flexible on those big films and learn to compromise and find solutions quickly."

been a DoP for a long time, I am very specific in my instruction. If they have different opinions, I will listen and respect their choices.

After all these years working with cinematographers, there is one thing I insist on and that is that they give the actors more space and time. I won't allow them to spend more than two hours preparing the lighting and camera. Especially during the changing of scenes, if the crew takes too long, the actors' performance may not be consistent and continuous. You can't keep the actor waiting too long.

I also insist that the cinematographer not interfere too much with the performances. It's quite normal for him to ask actors to look to one side when they start speaking or walk to a certain corner before they start acting, but if they request too much from the actors, I step in and ask them to stop—or I ask the actors to ignore

their requests. I want the actors to concentrate on acting and not be distracted by technical matters.

Most crew who have worked with me before understand what I mean in this regard all too well. I think, with the advent of digital cameras, which allows us to use sometimes more than five cameras, it's become even harder to keep the performances of the actors continuous.

What I ask from the cinematographers is to use his technical and artistic skills to serve the characters in the story.

In general I don't shoot a lot of coverage, although it does depend on the needs of each project. In the opening scene of **Not One Less**, for example—where we were trying to present a realistic picture of the village, but dealing with so many kids who knew nothing about acting—we shot 15,000 feet of film in just one day. And on a large action scene, we sometimes use five ›

cameras at the same time. But in general, if we shoot too much footage, I would start to worry and try to control the situation.

I don't particularly care about the size of a project. It has to be about the story. If the scale of the story is big and complicated, naturally the budget is bigger. In a way it has become a routine that I shoot something small and simple after a big action-related film. For me it's a way to find a balance and enliven the creative process. It's important for me to switch my mind to something different. We should always look at simple stories. I think in everyone's heart, there is a desire to return to innocence.

As a filmmaker, your eyes shouldn't be blurred by anything other than telling the story. You shouldn't be distracted by the thought of winning awards or making money or getting bigger budgets. Human emotions and human nature are the focus of everything.

Today, I think filmmakers in China face double pressure. First, your film has to be profound and meaningful and second, it has to be entertaining and have the potential to make money at the box office. These two goals are often contradictory, but we have no other way than to work harder on that. Filmmakers have to reach both goals at the same time so that our film industry can develop under normal circumstances.

You could say that my whole life has been in pursuit of a balance between strong, profound filmmaking and entertaining, profit-making cinema. Maybe **The Flowers of War** can achieve that balance.

I don't like to think I am such a deep thinker. I don't like films to be too difficult for audiences. I don't want to make films like that and I don't think I would be able to. I always wanted to make films for the public, for the common man, and make the films enjoyable. I have never pretended to be a deep thinker. ,,

01 Zhang with Wei Minzhi, the non-professional actor who landed the leading role in **Not One Less**

02 Zhang directing the village children in **Not One Less**

03 **Not One Less**

THE FLOWERS OF WAR

(04–06) Zhang's latest film, **The Flowers of War**, is one of the most expensive films to be made in China to date, with a budget of about $90m. In Mandarin and English, and featuring Oscar-winning US/UK actor Christian Bale in a key role, the film is based on Yan Geling's novel *The 13 Woman Of Nanjing*, the tragic story of thirteen Chinese prostitutes who volunteered as sex slaves for the Japanese soldiers who had invaded Nanjing in 1937.

"I bought the film rights in 2007," says Zhang. "The Nanjing massacre has been featured in various films, TV dramas and books before and every two years or so there is another film or TV program coming out about it. But when I read the novel, I felt that it was an unconventional story about the subject. That is what I found interesting. I didn't want to make a serious historical film about Nanjing because there would be too many restrictions, including the concern about the Sino-Japanese relationship and the danger of raising nationalistic emotions. Yan Geling's novel to me was like a faint mist of pink color amid the cruelty and brutality, and that kind of feeling to me was very artistic. It's a unique story about human nature and humanity. I don't want to challenge the perspective of that part of history nor create a new interpretation of history. I don't think a film director should emphasize perspectives anyway; a filmmaker is not a philosopher nor a historian."

The film is taken from the point of view of a 13-year-old girl, which differs from the novel. "We are trying to depict the 'pink' through the eyes of this little girl," says Zhang. "People are still making films about World War II and the Holocaust in the west, because those stories talk about humanity or express the beauty of humanity. This is what really interests me."

The film is the most expensive in Chinese cinema to date, a fact that put more pressure on Zhang when he was making it.

"It was a real test of the filmmaker's strength and preparation to handle such a huge production and complicated teamwork," he explains. "It was a great learning experience for me as a director, but also for the crew. We brought in Joss Williams [the visual effects supervisor whose credits include **The Pacific** and **Green Zone**] to help the crew out with explosions. The death and injury rate from explosion work has been very high in Chinese cinema and TV so hopefully we are becoming more professional and can reduce this."

04–05 Zhang directing newcomer Ni Ni in **The Flowers of War**

06 Zhang and Christian Bale discussing a scene in **The Flowers of War**

Akira Kurosawa

Akira Kurosawa (1910–1998) may have sparked a worldwide appreciation for Japanese cinema with his 1950 classic **Rashomon**, but the thirty-two films he directed, spanning over fifty years, are some of the greatest the world has ever seen, encompassing legendary titles such as **Ikiru** (1952), **Seven Samurai** (1954), **Throne of Blood** (1957), **Yojimbo** (1961) and **Ran** (1985). Known for his compassion and humanism, his visual flair and pioneering technique, and his absorption in and command of every aspect of the filmmaking craft from writing to editing, he is a much-cited influence for most of today's great directors.

Born in 1910 in Tokyo, Kurosawa showed an early talent for painting and enrolled in art school at the age of 17, but failing to make a living out of his passion, he answered a recruitment ad from a film studio seeking assistant directors. He secured a position as an assistant to director Kajurô Yamamoto in 1936 and worked for him for five years, eventually writing and directing on the Yamamoto films himself. His first feature **Sanshiro Sugata** (1943) was successful with audiences

and critics although the Japanese censors considered it too "British–American"—a controversial assertion in those war years—and had 18 minutes cut from it.

Although he started making films every year after that, it wasn't until the war ended that Kurosawa started to deliver extraordinary work like **Drunken Angel** (1948), which broke through conventions of narrative, casting, music and subject matter. The film was gritty, hard-hitting and subversive, and featured a powerful performance from dynamic newcomer Toshirô Mifune in the role of a gangster with tuberculosis. Kurosawa and Mifune would go on to make sixteen films together.

Stray Dog (1949) continued to show Kurosawa's bravura in its depiction of post-war Tokyo, blending real footage of the war-ravaged city into its narrative, but his career took a dramatic turn with **Rashomon** (1950), the famous story of a murder and rape told from multiple viewpoints, which won the Golden Lion at the 1951 Venice Film Festival and was a surprise

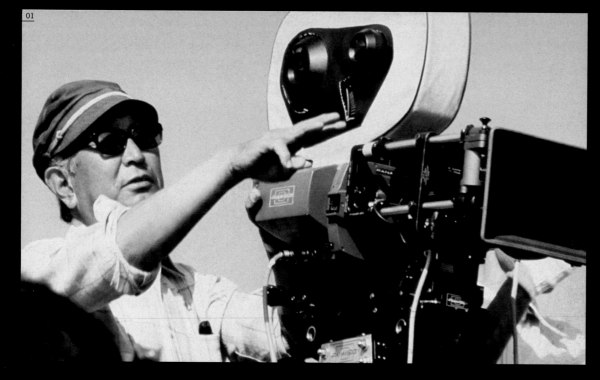

01

01 Akira Kurosawa

his visual flair and pioneering technique,
and his absorption in and command of every
aspect of the filmmaking craft from writing
to editing, he is a much-cited influence
for most of today's great directors."

03

05

commercial success in the US. **Rashomon**
kick-started a vogue for Japanese film; it also
coined a phrase now widely adopted to describe
the subjective perception of recollection.

A golden period followed in Kurosawa's career
with films such as **Ikiru**, a satirical drama about a
bureaucrat dying of cancer, and **Seven Samurai**,
the director's first true epic, which took over a
year in pre-production and production. Using
long lenses and multiple cameras, Kurosawa
created some of the most memorable battle
sequences ever shot in the story of a poor village
that hires a group of Samurai to protect it against
bandits. The film would of course be remade in
Hollywood six years later as **The Magnificent
Seven** (1960).

He adapted Shakespeare (**Throne of Blood** is
his version of **Macbeth**) and Gorky (**The Lower
Depths**), made a huge commercial hit in the
adventure movie **The Hidden Fortress** (1958),
tackled the samurai again in the violent
Yojimbo—which Sergio Leone remade as **Fistful
of Dollars** (1964)—and its sequel **Sanjuro**
(1962), and delivered humanist classics in **High**

Kurosawa struggled to maintain his pace over
the next fifteen years. He flirted unsuccessfully
with a Hollywood film and, unable to secure local
funding, he attempted suicide in 1971. He
returned to the screen courtesy of Russian
funding with **Dersu Uzala** (1975), about the clash
between nature and civilization in Siberia, but
even after that film won the Oscar for best foreign
language film, he was still unable to attract
money back in Japan.

On hearing of his troubles, young US
filmmakers George Lucas and Francis Ford
Coppola helped him source finance from 20th
Century Fox for the 16th-century war epic
Kagemusha (1980), which went on to win the
Palme d'Or at Cannes. His last great film in
1985—and one of the greatest in his career—was
Ran, a thrilling, monumental saga about a feuding
warlord family that was loosely based on **King
Lear**. At that time the most expensive production
ever mounted in Japan, it was a thematically rich,
visually magnificent film, and a fitting testament
to Kurosawa's mastery of craft. After **Ran**, he
made three more not-so-memorable films before

Glossary

24 frames per second
The standard frame rate for film, a frame being a single image produced by the camera.

35mm
The standard film format used today in which the filmstrip is 35mm wide.

Alexa
The Alexa is a digital film camera manufactured by Arri that first came to market in 2010.

Assistant director
The director's right-hand person who traditionally takes over the routine functions on set to allow the director to focus on the creative direction of the film. The AD is responsible for keeping track of the schedule, and keeping order and quiet on a set, among many other functions and often has his own assistants known as ''first'' and ''second.''

Clapperboard
A device (traditionally a pair of hinged boards) that is clapped together before or after each take to mark when camera and sound are running synchronously.

Close-up
A shot that focuses on an actor's face or is close enough to an object that not much of the background or surrounding imagery can be seen.

Coverage
The process of shooting a particular scene from all the necessary angles so that there's enough flexibility to cut between different shots and have all the footage necessary for post-production.

Crane shot
A shot taken from a hydraulic device that lifts the camera off the ground, often allowing for sweeping or majestic shots.

Dailies
The footage from the previous day's shooting, which allows the director and cinematographer to gauge performances, light, color, and other concerns while the film is being shot.

Dolly zoom (aka trombone effect)
A technique in which the camera moves closer or further from the subject while simultaneously adjusting the zoom angle to keep the subject the same size and stationary in the frame. The effect, famously used in

Vertigo and Jaws for example, keeps the subject stationary while the background changes.

Executive producer
A person who is responsible for bringing finance or key elements to the film, but who is not responsible for the day-to-day production activities and shooting. An executive producer could be an executive at the company behind the film or a distributor.

Focus puller
The member of the camera team who adjusts focus during a shot so that the correct person or object can be seen clearly at any one time.

Handheld camera
A camera that is not bolted down to any device, such as a dolly or tripod, but is instead being held by the camera operator. This technique is often incorporated to create a more realistic, looser, more spontaneous and emotionally charged sensation in the viewer.

Jump cut
An abrupt cut within a scene in which a section of film is cut from a movement or the camera is stopped and restarted when the subject is in a different position. The effect is used for stylistic reasons—perhaps most famously in Jean-Luc Godard's **Breathless**—and was once considered a travesty by those who favoured continuity editing.

Long lens
A lens with an angle of view narrower than that of the human eye.

Long shot
A shot that encompasses much of the background. The camera is at a distance from the actors, allowing the characters to be surrounded by their environment.

Mise-en-scène
A French expression describing the style of a director, from how everything appears on set to the positioning and movement of the actors to the lighting.

Panavision cameras
Panavision is an equipment manufacturer specializing in cameras and lenses, which originally specialized in widescreen lenses, but grew to develop other lenses and cameras, both film and digital.

Red Camera
The Red One is a 4K digital camera that first went on the market in 2007 and has been widely used in feature film production by advocate directors such as Steven Soderbergh, Peter Jackson and David Fincher.

Storyboard
A drawing that gives a blueprint for how an image (or a series of images) should look through the viewfinder. Directors and cinematographers will use storyboards to help illustrate their ideas before going on set to block a shot.

Super 8 camera
8mm is traditionally a home movie format in which the filmstrip is 8mm wide: there are standard 8mm and Super 8 formats, the difference being that Super 8 has a larger image area.

Tracking shot
A moving camera shot that follows along with the characters through space.

Wide-angle lens
A lens that projects a larger image circle than a standard lens, that can handle wider fields of view, create perspective distortion or enable large shift movements.

Picture Credits

Alamy/Photos 12: 38B.

Courtesy of Pedro Almodóvar/Illustration by Juan Gatti: 18CR, 18T, 18BR, 19TR, 19TL.

Courtesy of Olivier Assayas: 25, 26T, 28, 30T, 31T, 32T, 33B.

Courtesy of the Austrian Film Museum/Copyright Michael Haneke: 134, 138, 141T, 141BL.

Courtesy of Nuri Bilge Ceylan: 46, 49, 50, 51, 53, 54, 55.

Courtesy of Park Chan-wook/Storyboard by the Conti Brothers (team name), Zoohan Cha (lead artist): 154, 155.

Corbis/Sunset Boulevard: 93B.

Courtesy of Jean-Pierre Dardenne and Luc Dardenne: 61, 63T.

Egg Films/Show East: 150.

© Film en Stock/Jean-Claude Moireau: 26B, 27B, 27T.

El Deseo/Renn/France 2: 16BL, 16CL.

Courtesy of Terry Gilliam/Storyboards by Terry Gilliam for Brazil: 104, 106, 109.

Courtesy of Amos Gitai/www.amosgitai.com: 112, 115, 116, 117, 118, 119, 120, 121T.

Doane Gregory: 39.

The Kobal Collection: 76TL, 110, 156, 164; 20th Century Fox: 77 L; 20th Century Fox/Universal: 172CL, 172BL, 172T; 20th Century Fox/Universal/Stephen Vaughan: 173; Agav Hafakot/MP Prod/Canal+: 121B; Alliance Atlantis: 159TL, 159BL; Alpha Films: 180BR; Anouchka/Orsay: 111L; Arcade/Arena Films/Cab/Canal+/Cnc:31BL, 31BR; Archipel 35/Films du Fleuve/RTBF: 60; BAC Films: 114; BBC/Celador Productions: 96TR; BBC/Celador Productions/Laurie Sparham: 96CR, 96BR; Beijing Film Studios/China Film Corporation/Hero China International/Wide River Investments: 184; Beijing New Picture Film Co.: 176; Beijing New Picture Film Co./Sony pictures Classics/Bai Xiaoyan: 181T, 181B, 182BR; Beijing New Picture/Elite Group: 181R (top 3), 184; Canal+ Espana: 68B; Canal+ Espana/Miguel Bracho: 68T; Canal+/MK2/Arte France: 135; Canal+/Sony Pictures/Christine Plenus: 59; Castle Rock/Malpaso/Columbia/Graham Kuhn: 78; CCC/Hungarofilm/ZDF: 161TR; China Film Group Corporation/Bai Xiaoyan: 180CL, 180BL, 185TL, 185TR; Cineplex Odeon: 76T; CJ Ent/Intz Com/KTB Network: 146; CJ Entertainment/Studio Box: 152; Columbia TriStar: 186B; Columbia/Tri-Star: 72; Dacia Films: 30BR, 30BL; Daien: 189BR; Daniel Martinez: 21BR; Dreamworks SKG/Warner Bros: 85; Dreamworks/Doane Gregory: 40, 41; Eastcroft/Low Key Productions/Francois Duhamel: 98; Egg Films/Show East: 148, 149; El Desea-Lauren: 14; El Deseo S.A.: 12, 15TR, 15B, 15TL, 18BL, 19C, 19BL; El Deseo/Jorge Aparicio: 21T; El Deseo/Miguel Bracho: 17T, 17B; El Deseo/Renn/France 2: 16T, 16CR, 16BR; Enterprise Pictures: 163; Era International: 180T, 182TR, 182CR; Era/Shanghai Film Studio: 183; Film Fyn: 42, 43; Focus Features: 155BR, 155 TR; Handmade Films: 102; Herald Ace/Nippon Herald/Greenwich: 189T; Iguana/Ventana/Imcine: 67; Imagine Entertainment: 82T; Imagine Entertainment/Universal: 83; ITV Global: 45BL, 125; ITV Global/Bernard Walsh: 124; Journeyman Films Ltd.: 24; Lucky Red: 63B, 63C; Mafilm: 158; Mafilm/Mokep/ZDF: 161CL; Mafilm/Studio Objectiv: 162; Malpaso Productions: 88; Margo Films: 22, 32B; MGM: 143T; MGM/UA: 175; Miramax: 97TL; Miramax/Kerry Hayes: 70; MK2 Productions: 29; New Line/Bruce Talamon: 71; October Films/Christine Plenus: 56; October Films/Studio Canal+/Filmsdu Fleuve/Christine Plenus: 62; Palm Pictures: 33T; Paramount: 143B, 168T, 170; Paramount/Melinda Sue Gordon: 168BR, 168BL, 169T; Parnassus Production: 108, 109CR, 109TR, 109CL, 109BL; Picnic/BEF/Australian Film Commission: 174; Polygram/Phillip Caruso: 107; Prominent Features/Sergio Strizzi: 106T; Python Pictures/EMI: 101TL, 101TR; RKO: 76TR; Rome-Paris/De Laurentiis/Beauregard: 111L; Serendipity/Hogarth/Myriad/Alex Dukay: 160; Sil-Metropole: 182L; Sony Pictures: 136, 137; Studio Canal+/Centre National de la Cinematographie: 132, 140TL; Sveriges Television/Bengt Wanselius: 44; Tartan Films: 144, 153; Tequila Gang/WB: 6, 69; Tesauro/Ana Muller: 21BL; Toho: 189BC; Toho/Kurosawa: 188, 189BL; Tokuma Enterprises: 182C; Touchstone: 171B; Touchstone/Bonnie Schiffman: 171T; Umbrella: 101B; United Artists: 77R; Universal: 103T, 103CR, 127TR, 127CL, 128T, 128BR, 129TL, 129TR, 131BL, 131BR, 142; Universal International Pictures: 5, 20; Universal Pictures: 2, 64, 73, 75L, 122; Universal/Embassy: 105; Universal/Jasin Boland: 128BL, 129B, 131T; Universal/Jonathan Olley: 127TL, 127CR, 127B; Universal/Peter Mountain: 103CL, 103B; Warner Bros: 76B, 80, 81, 82C, 82B, 87BR, 89, 94, 97BL, 166; Warner Bros/Merie W. Wallace: 84, 86, 87BL, 87T; Warner Brothers Pictures Espana: 75TR, 75BR; WDR/RMF/MIDA/Diaphama/BBC/Melissa Moseley: 90; Wega Film:138BL, 138BR, 138CL, 139; Working Title/Channel 4: 93T; X-Filme Creative Pool: 140T, 140C, 140B, 141BR; Xi'an Film Studio: 179; Zentropa: 38T, 37T, 37B; Zentropa/Two Brothers: 34.

Courtesy of Seung-yong Lim/Storyboard by Sang-yong Jung: 151.

Frank Masi: 97BR.

Rex Features/SNAP: 45TL, 45R.

Courtesy of István Szabó: 159R, 161BR, 161BL.

Courtesy of Peter Weir: 167, 169B, 172BR, 172CR.

Courtesy of Zhang Yimou/Photograph by Bai Xiaoyan: 181BR, 185BL, 185BR, 186TL, 186TR, 187.

Special thanks to Caroline Bailey, Darren Thomas, Cheryl Thomas, Dave Kent and Phil Moad and at The Kobal Collection for all of their effort and support.

Every effort has been made to acknowledge pictures. However, the publisher apologizes if there are any unintentional omissions.